Bible essentials you just need to know...

DIGGING DEEP

BIBLE STUDY MADE EASY

46 ENGAGING TOPICS

Segun Ibitoye

Digging Deep - Bible Study Made Easy

Copyright © 2017 by Olusegun Victor Ibitoye

First Printing 2017

All rights reserved. This book or parts thereof may not be copied, edited, reproduced or transmitted in any form or by any means, electronic, mechanical, or otherwise, without prior written permission of the copyright owner.

Scripture taken from the Holy Bible, New International Version®, NIV® Copyright ©1973, 1978, 1984, 2011 by Biblica, Inc.® Used by permission. All rights reserved.

Extracts from the Authorized Version of the Bible (The King James Bible), the rights which are vested in the crown, are produced by permission of the Crown's Patentee, Cambridge University Press.

Scripture quotations marked KJV are taken from The King James Version of the Bible.

Digging Deep - Bible Study Made Easy by Segun Ibitoye
Published in the UK & Africa by A God So Near Publications
> ISBN 978-0-9926878-1-6 (Paperback)
> ISBN 978-0-9926878-2-3 (Hardback)
> ISBN 978-0-9926878-3-0 (Ebook)

Cover Design & Book Layout by Segun Ibitoye
Back Cover photograph by Andrew Franklin Photography
Edited by Kathy Kehrli, The Flawless Word, USA
Printed in the United Kingdom
Website: **www.diggingdeep.guru**

Dedication

I dedicate this book to all bible scholars who are impatiently desirous of knowledge and to the selfless men and women of God who seek, commend, and spread knowledge.

Acknowledgements

There are times when our efforts bring no profit. Just like Simon, the fisherman, you may have worked hard all night long and have not caught a thing. If you have not thrown away your net, and with Christ by your side, there is hope. When next you let down the net into deep water you may catch more fish than you ever dreamed possible. So be willing to try again.

Words of wisdom are likened to sharp sticks that shepherds use to guide sheep, and they have been given by God, the one Shepherd of us all. I thank the Almighty God for continually inspiring me to write, invent, and publish despite lack of incentive. Of a truth, "time and chance happen to them all" and "there is no end to the writing of books."

In the path charted for me by God stood three meek and gifted prophets of God in the Celestial Church of Christ. I have received God's guidance from them at no cost. To my fathers-in-the-Lord, Superior Evangelist Richard Moronfolu, Superior Evangelist Anthony Emmanuel, and Superior Evangelist Olushola Ogunleye, I feel a sense of gratitude. I pray that your ministries will grow luxuriantly until the coming of our Lord, Jesus Christ.

If there is a friend who sticks closer than a brother, there is a wife who is like a mother. To Adetola, my wife, you are like a merchant ship. Were we blessed with a ship, I would have named it MT *Adetola*.

To all the inquiring bible scholars, I welcome your inquisitiveness for it spurred me a great deal. Just as Simon allowed the Chief Shepherd to use his boat to teach, be willing to use your talent and vocational tools in the Lord's service.

Contents

1. A Preamble — 1
2. Betrayal — 6
3. Attempting Something Perceived as Too Difficult — 15
4. Impossible Is Unbelief — 16
5. Regarding Curses — 24
6. Concerning Spiritual Gifts — 32
7. Demand What Is Yours — 41
8. Don't be Sluggish; Act Quickly — 43
9. Integrity — 44
10. How Do I Answer? — 46
11. The Power in Praise — 50
12. Bad Company Corrupts — 60
13. Vessels unto Honour — 71
14. Ark of the Covenant — 76
15. Taming the Tongue — 82
16. What Adversaries Do to Hinder Work — 96
17. God's Timing — 104
18. Fruit of the Spirit — 108
19. Hezekiah's Achievements and Mistakes — 116
20. Understanding Prophecy — 122

Contents

21 Jonah's Expectation --------------------------------------- 133

22 A Scriptural Guide to a Successful Business ------------- 139

23 Dealing Wisely -- 148

24 Contentment -- 160

25 Opportunity: Sense It & Grab It --------------------------- 165

26 Obedience --- 176

27 Wisdom -- 185

28 Faith --- 195

29 Humility -- 204

30 Dealing with Anger --------------------------------------- 211

31 Forgiveness --- 217

32 Making Vows -- 220

33 Moral Maxims 1 (Proverbs 25) ----------------------------- 225

34 Moral Maxims 2 (Proverbs 26) ----------------------------- 230

35 Moral Maxims 3 (Proverbs 27) ----------------------------- 234

36 Moral Maxims 4 (Proverbs 28) ----------------------------- 240

37 Moral Maxims 5 (Proverbs 29) ----------------------------- 245

38 A Virtuous Woman (Proverbs 31) -------------------------- 250

39 A Good Husband -- 256

40 Jealousy --- 260

Contents

41 Revenge --- 264
42 Is There Punishment for Our Sins? ---------------------- 268
43 The Grace of Giving -- 272
44 The Enemy's Tactics --------------------------------------- 277
45 How to Please God --- 288
46 Is Your Faith in Downturn?--- ---------------------------- 291
47 Will the Almighty Pervert Justice?------------------------ 295
48 God's Team Working --------------------------------------- 300
49 Is Your Pastor or Shepherd a Joshua?------------------- 306
50 Jesus Knows You by Name ------------------------------- 314
51 Army Without Weapons ----------------------------------- 320
52 Spiritual Gym --- 327
53 Change of Nationality ------------------------------------- 331
54 Why I Don't Like God... ----------------------------------- 334

> "Then he opened their minds so they could understand the Scriptures."
>
> - Luke 24:45

A Preamble

It may be difficult to understand an act of disloyalty or unfaithfulness until you are personally involved as the victim of the betrayal or the betrayer. It may also be impossible to go through life without experiencing such infidelity. This book seeks to make the reader dig deep into the scriptures to find out and understand significant actions that can alter a person's life or circumstances in a substantial way. Such actions also include curses and acting promptly to prevent loss or to make gains. Those things that happened in biblical times can still happen now - there is no new thing under the sun.

Think of mineral exploration. You do not scratch the surface of the earth to get a diamond, one of the world's most expensive minerals. You dig deep. According to www.mining-technology.com, "The operating depth at Mponeng gold mine ranged from between 2.4 km to more than 3.9 km below the surface by the end of 2012. Ongoing expansions have resulted in deeper digging at Mponeng, pushing the record to beyond the four kilometer mark." Similarly, reading a few verses of the scriptures may not be enough to reveal those invaluable life-changing lessons that this book seeks to point out to readers. Again, you will need to dig deep for those lessons that are able to make you wise, help you avoid pitfalls, and train you to do all kinds of good deeds. The good news is that you've got one of the right tools (this book) to dig deep in your hands this very minute.

As a Christian whose duties include winning souls for Jesus Christ and doing good for the sake of the gospel, are you prepared, or would you be more likely to take an evasive action when asked a question about your faith? An opportunity to teach an inquiring mind about the good news and Jesus Christ should never be missed. This book will prepare you to preach, teach, and answer questions about not only the bible but also the various positive, life-changing subjects contained in it that are usually discussed during bible study.

If you teach in the bible class, or you intend to do so in the future, it can be challenging. You may sometimes be asked questions that will make you scan your brain quickly for answers. Although you are led by the Holy Spirit, it is likely that you will fumble through your reply. For example, a young man once stopped me unexpectedly to ask this question:

> *"If God is good, why did he confuse the language of the people building the Tower of Babel?"*

To respond effectively, I allowed other scholars to have a go. Following my lead will afford you time to think. It will also give you an idea of some of the scholars' level of understanding of the question posed. Now, to answer the question above, look at the instructions in Genesis 8:17 and Genesis 9:1,7. Then relate these mandates to the intentions of the people building the Tower of Babel in Genesis 11:4. It will also be good to establish that God is supreme (greatest in power and authority). Read Psalm 115:3.

Apart from that question above, there are many questions in this book that can stimulate interest or discussion during bible study, and each of them deserves an answer. 'A curious child is a teacher's delight,' they say. If scholars do not ask questions, then the teacher should so as to embolden them. Sincerely, I have never come across an unquestioning bible scholar or teacher.

After Jesus told his disciples the parable of the Net, he posed a question:

> *"'Have you understood all these things?' Jesus asked. 'Yes,' they replied."* - Matthew 13:51

If you are thinking of teaching in a bible class or converting souls to follow Christ, then use the words of the Psalmist as a yardstick. He was quite knowledgeable about God and had an idea of how to be prepared. In Psalm 51, he requested five things, highlighted in bold in the bible quotation directly below, before he could teach.

> *"Create in me **a pure heart**, O God, and renew **a steadfast spirit** within me. Do not cast me from your presence or take your **Holy Spirit** from me. Restore to me **the joy of your salvation** and grant me **a willing spirit**, to sustain me. Then I will teach transgressors your ways, so that sinners will turn back to you."* - Psalm 51:10-13

This is noteworthy - a considerable number of qualities are acquirable if only you have a willing spirit (i.e., you are willing to obey God). Clearly, anyone wishing to be instructed by God must repent at his rebuke. Take a look at Proverbs 1:23:

> *"If you had responded to my rebuke, I would have poured out my heart to you and made my thoughts known to you."*

Keep in mind this promise in Psalm 84:11:

> *"Our Lord and our God, you are like the sun and also like a shield. You treat us with kindness and with honour, **never denying any good thing to those who live right**."*

People often ask, "Will studying the bible bring you success?" Yes, I would say. But you will have to continually make the effort to observe everything you are being exposed to (Joshua 1:8). When you do, you will be "like someone who dug down deep and built a house on solid rock" as described in Luke 6:47-48. Continue to do the same thing when you are successful. Only then will you achieve genuine greatness. People like King David and King Hezekiah had great success, and the Lord was with Joseph so that he was successful in whatever he did. These biblical men were just as human as we are, but was the scripture available to Joseph?

There are over forty-six bible study topics in this book that you can use as a study guide. The content features *new materials* plus expanded and revised previously published ones from my books, *A King Needs This - Bible Study Made Easy* and *A Queen Needs This - Bible Study Made Easy*. I am delighted to offer readers, in a single edition, this 'trilogy' of bible study materials that I have developed over the course of a decade.

For ease of understanding, this book, like my other books, is written in plain language, thus making it pleasurable to read. Reading it with a bible beside you, which you can refer to, makes it an even more enjoyable read. This witty approach is a ploy to make the reader study the bible, and if it is successful, then I am encouraged.

As you read this book, may God fill you with the knowledge of his will. May he suffuse you with all the wisdom and understanding his Spirit gives so that you will be able to do what pleases Him. Amen.

Betrayal

Only a loner may not be betrayed for he or she avoids the company of other people. But if you keep the company of others, occupy an important position, or are influential, then a servant, a counsellor, a son, a daughter, or a lover may betray you. The question is, can you avoid such disloyalty?

A good look at the scripture provides insight into this topic. Let us consider these biblical characters:

Ziba, a servant of Saul's household. Read 2 Samuel 9, 2 Samuel 15, 2 Samuel 16:1-4, and 2 Samuel 19:9-30.

Ahithophel, one of King David's trusted counsellors. Read 1 Chronicles 27:33, 2 Samuel 15:10-12, 30-36, 2 Samuel 16:15-23, and 2 Samuel 17:1-23.

Absalom, the guy who conspired against his father, David. Read 2 Samuel 3:1-5, 2 Samuel 13:28, 2 Samuel 15, and 2 Samuel 18:9-18.

Delilah, Samson's lover. Read Judges 16:1-21. Also look at Proverbs 7:21-27.

Judas Iscariot, the man who betrayed Jesus. Read Matthew 26:14, John 13:2, Mark 14:43-51, and Matthew 27:1-6.

This character, Judas, tops them all and his disloyalty shows that anyone can be betrayed. Like Jesus, you might have seen it coming.

In relation to each of the biblical characters above, please answer the questions below. Unless you are familiar with the aforementioned biblical characters, it would be best to study the bible verses referred to above before attempting to answer the questions.

1. How did the betrayer carry out his/her scheme?

2. What was the motive behind each person's action?

3. Examine the relationship between the betrayer and the victim? Please also read Psalm 55:12-14.

4. What are the signs to watch out for? Tip: Sometimes they appear respectable, nice, and warm.

5. Is betrayal inevitable?

6. What end awaits a betrayer?

If it is possible, discuss this topic in your bible study class. The dialogue is usually gripping.

Let's start with Ziba, a servant of King Saul's household. Just as Joseph was in charge of Potiphar's house, King David gave Ziba charge over what was left of Saul's household. In fact, all the members of Ziba's household were servants of Mephibosheth, Saul's grandson.

> "I have given your master's grandson everything that belonged to Saul and his family. You and your sons and your servants are to farm the land for him and bring in the crops, so that your master's grandson may be provided for. And Mephibosheth, grandson of your master, will always eat at my table." - 2 Samuel 9:9-10

Considering that Absalom was vengeful, and that history was not on Mephibosheth's side because he was Saul's grandson, an opportunity came for Ziba to betray Mephibosheth when King David fled from Absalom. At this point, did Ziba think that Absalom's conspiracy against King David would consume Mephibosheth? Ziba took with him his fifteen sons and twenty servants, leaving Mephibosheth behind. He brought food for David's men to eat and wine for those who may have been exhausted. Notice that Ziba did not come empty-handed; he provided essentials to replenish stock for an army on the move. What a schemer Ziba was. He wanted to show King David he cared more than Mephibosheth.

When Ziba met King David, the king asked,

> "Where is your master's grandson?" Ziba said to him, "He is staying in Jerusalem, because he thinks, 'Today the Israelites will restore to me my grandfather's kingdom.'" - 2 Samuel 16:1-3

Really! Was that Mephibosheth's thought? To establish betrayal, let us hear what Mephibosheth said when King David returned to Jerusalem after the death of Absalom.

"Why didn't you go with me, Mephibosheth?" King David asked. Mephibosheth replied thus:

> "My lord the king, since I your servant am lame, I said, 'I will have my donkey saddled and will ride on it, so I can go with the king.' But Ziba my servant betrayed me. [27] And he has slandered your servant to my lord the king. My lord the king is like an angel of God; so do whatever you wish..." - 2 Samuel 19:24-28

Absalom made himself king in Hebron and to strengthen his rebellion, he invited Ahithophel, David's counselor. Should Ahithophel have gone to see Absalom? Although 200 men from Jerusalem were with Absalom, they had no idea that Absalom was planning a rebellion against his father.

When Absalom asked Ahithophel for advice, he said:

> "...Sleep with your father's concubines whom he left to take care of

> the palace. Then all Israel will hear that you have made yourself obnoxious to your father, and the hands of everyone with you will be more resolute." - 2 Samuel 16:21

If an advice is a recommendation as to the appropriate choice of action to take when you need to solve a problem, does humiliating one's father count as an advice? Especially since the advice came from someone who, in the past, gave such good advice that King David and Absalom thought it came straight from God?

Now, listen to the next advice coming from Ahithophel:

> "Ahithophel said to Absalom, 'I would choose twelve thousand men and set out tonight in pursuit of David. ² I would attack him while he is weary and weak. I would strike him with terror, and then all the people with him will flee. I would strike down only the king ³ and bring all the people back to you. The death of the man you seek will mean the return of all; all the people will be unharmed.' ⁴ This plan seemed good to Absalom and to all the elders of Israel."
> - 2 Samuel 17:1-4

It was good advice but observe carefully how Ahithophel personalized the plan using the word 'I' four times. It also arouses great interest because Ahithophel was not enlisted in Israel's army, although his son, Eliam, was one of David's Thirty Strongmen (2 Samuel 23:34).

Now, compare Ahithophel's advice to how Joseph advised Pharaoh after he interpreted Pharaoh's dream.

> "And now let Pharaoh **look for a discerning and wise man** and put him in charge of the land of Egypt." - Genesis 41:33

It would be right to conclude that Ahithophel advised Absalom in the manner he did because he had an ulterior motive. That is, to become King. Still not convinced, why would Ahithophel commit suicide just because Absalom and the leaders of Israel did not follow his (Ahithophel's) advice?

It is essential to pray. "Now David had been told, 'Ahithophel is among the conspirators with Absalom.' So David prayed, 'Lord, turn Ahithophel's counsel into foolishness.'" - 2 Samuel 15:31

Just as the Lord promised David in Psalm 89:22, the enemy did not outwit David. Also read Psalm 55. (What do you think of verses 20-21?)

To be relevant and so as to steal the hearts of the people of Israel, Absalom did two things. First, he cajoled anyone who came with a complaint to be placed before King David for a decision.

> "...Absalom would say to him, 'Look, your claims are valid and proper, but there is no representative of the king to hear you.' 4 And

> *Absalom would add, 'If only I were appointed judge in the land! Then everyone who has a complaint or case could come to me and I would see that they receive justice.'* - 2 Samuel 15:1-4

Second, whenever anyone approached Absalom to bow down before him, Absalom would reach out his hand, take hold of him, and kiss him. Four years later, Absalom left for Hebron and set himself up as king there.

Absalom's plan worked but couldn't King David have acted within those four years? A timely effort will prevent more work later, they say.

In the case of Delilah, the woman whom Samson fell in love with, betrayal was induced.

> "The rulers of the Philistines went to her and said, 'See if you can lure him into showing you the secret of his great strength and how we can overpower him so we may tie him up and subdue him. Each one of us will give you eleven hundred shekels of silver.'"
>
> - Judges 16:5

Now that Delilah has been enticed with money, she did exactly what the rulers of the Philistines requested by asking Samson to tell her the secret of his great strength and how he could be tied up and subdued. But Samson made a fool of her thrice by telling her a fib each time.

> "...*With such nagging she prodded him day after day until he was sick to death of it.* [17] *"So he told her everything. 'No razor has ever been used on my head,' he said, 'because I have been a Nazirite dedicated to God from my mother's womb. If my head were shaved, my strength would leave me, and I would become as weak as any other man.'"* - Judges 16:6-17

Delilah sent for the Philistines once she had put Samson to sleep, and someone shaved off the seven braids of his hair and his strength left him.

Betrayers do not all belong to the same stratum; unlike Delilah, Judas Iscariot, a designated apostle of Jesus Christ, went to the chief priests and asked,

> "...'*What are you willing to give me if I deliver him over to you?' So they counted out for him thirty pieces of silver. From then on Judas watched for an opportunity to hand him over.*"
>
> - Matthew 26:14-15

The opportunity came and it was sealed with a kiss (Matthew 26:47-49).

Out of the five betrayers mentioned above, Ahithophel and Judas

Iscariot committed suicide. Three javelins were plunged into Absalom's heart by Joab when his hair got caught in the tree while riding his mule in battle in the forest of Ephraim. Ziba got part of Mephibosheth's land, and after subduing Samson, the rulers of the Philistines returned with silver in their hands to give to Delilah.

Remember this: "A person can receive only what is given them from heaven." - John 3:27

Attempting Something Perceived as Too Difficult

Take a look at the following characters in the bible:
Daniel (Daniel 2)

Esther and Mordecai (Esther 3 and Esther 4)

Elisha (2 Kings 6)

1. What difficult situation did each face?

2. For each character/case, what was at stake?

3. How did each person attempt to surmount the difficulty?

4. What ability did each one deploy?

5. How long did each have to react?

6. Was the expected outcome achieved by each one?

7. Were there benefits for each one's effort?

8. Who else benefited from their exploits?

Now, for answers to the questions above, please proceed to the next chapter, Impossible is Unbelief.

Impossible Is Unbelief

The company of the prophets went to the Jordan and began to cut down trees so as to build a bigger meeting place. While one of the prophets was working, the iron axe head fell into the water and he said to Elisha, "Oh no, my lord!" "It was borrowed!" The man who exclaimed that 'it was borrowed' thought it was impossible to retrieve the axe head and he may also have thought about the explanation he would to give for not returning the axe head to its owner. Elisha cut a stick and threw it there, and made the iron float. Did God have a reason to make it happen for Elisha? Yes. What Elisha did defied the science that deals with matter, energy, motion, and force.

Let us look at the intention of the company of the prophets and compare it with that of the people who set out to build the Tower of Babel. The place where the company of the prophets met with Elisha was too small and they wanted to build a bigger meeting place. Elisha said it was a good idea. Now compare that with the intention of the people who wanted to build the Tower of Babel; they wanted to make a name for themselves and they do not want to be scattered all over the world. Not wanting to be scattered all over the world is contradicting God's commandment in Genesis 1:28. Therefore, their intention was not good.

There are instances in the bible where individuals thought

certain pronouncements or prophecies cannot be fulfilled. But God always honour the pronouncement of his servants that does his will. In Joshua 6:26, Joshua pronounced this solemn oath:

> "Cursed before the Lord is the one who undertakes to rebuild this city, Jericho: "At the cost of his firstborn son he will lay its foundations; at the cost of his youngest he will set up its gates.""

Foolishly,

> "Hiel of Bethel rebuilt Jericho. He laid its foundations at the cost of his firstborn son Abiram, and he set up its gates at the cost of his youngest son Segub, in accordance with the word of the Lord spoken by Joshua son of Nun." - 1 Kings 16:34

One wonders if Joshua's pronouncement was not recorded for posterity. But if Hiel knew about Joshua's declaration, he must have thought it was impossible for that to happen.

When there was serve famine in Samaria, Elisha foretold relief in 2 Kings 7:1 -

> "Hear the word of the Lord. This is what the Lord says: About this time tomorrow, a seah of the finest flour will sell for a shekel and two seahs of barley for a shekel at the gate of Samaria."

But the officer on whose arm the king was leaning said to the man of God,

> "Look, even if the Lord should open the floodgates of the heavens, could this happen?"

Here, let us consider two things; the severity of the famine and the prophecy of the man of God promising relief within twenty four hours. But Elisha was a credible prophet of God whose prophecy should not be doubted. On the other hand, the officer may have thought that it takes about four months between planting and harvesting of barley. How would God do it in just twenty four hours? If God wanted barley planted and harvested within twenty four hours, it can be done. He did a similar thing before. When Moses placed the staffs of the leaders of the ancestral tribes of Israel before the Lord in the tent of the covenant law as instructed, Aaron's staff sprouted, budded, blossomed and produced almonds overnight (A process that usually last about five years). Read Number 17:6-9. It is worth noting that God and his team created man in a day. He also controls time.

So God works in mysterious ways. The same God who made Aaron's staff to bud overnight also controls sound. He caused the Arameans to hear the sound of chariots and horses and a great army. The Arameans ran way leaving behind their tents and their horses and donkeys. Afterwards, 'the people went out and plundered the camp of the Arameans. So a seah of the finest flour sold for a shekel, and two seahs of barley sold for a shekel, as the Lord had said.'

When the angel of the Lord told Zechariah, "...your prayer has been heard", one can conclude that having a child was something Zechariah considered possible (at the time he made the supplication to God). Read Luke 1:11-20. But God visited him when his wife and he were both very old. Did Zechariah think it was possible for him to father a child called John? There was an element of doubt. "How can I be sure of this?" he asked the angel of God.

Regarding child birth at old age, Abraham laughed (Genesis 17:17) when God told him that Sarah, his wife, will be the mother of nations and Sarah also laughed (Genesis 18:12) when of one the three men that visited Abraham said "I will surely return to you about this time next year, and Sarah your wife will have a son."

Is anything too hard for the Lord? The same God who blessed Abraham and Sarah with a son in their old age similarly blessed Zechariah and his wife with John.

When Goliath came out and challenged the army of Israel every morning and every evening for forty days, Saul and his men were so frightened of Goliath, the Philistine, that they couldn't do a thing until David showed up. By the battle lines, David heard about the reward for the man who kills this Philistine and removes disgrace from Israel; it was enough to induce David to take on Goliath. Was David's ability to take on Goliath doubted by his oldest brother, Eliab or was Eliab seriously concerned about the few sheep David left in the wilderness? Regarding the livestock, David had done the needful - 'David left the flock in the care of a shepherd'. Look at 1 Samuel 17:20-29.

Like fear, unbelief is infectious. But David knew his prowess and he told King Saul, who doubted his ability, how the Lord rescued him from the paw of the lion and the paw of the bear. Not only did David likened Goliath to the lion and the bear he killed, David psyched himself and he ran quickly toward the battle line to meet Goliath whom he killed.

When king Nebuchadnezzar summoned the magicians, enchanters, sorcerers and astrologers to tell him his dream and its interpretation, the astrologers said, *"There is no one on earth who can do what the king asks!"* Simply, they meant it was impossible. But there were four men in king Nebuchadnezzar's kingdom who were ten times better than all the magicians and enchanters. One of them, Daniel, could understand visions and dreams of all kinds. To accomplish the task, they need to know Nebuchadnezzar's dream before giving the meaning of the dream. Therefore, Daniel and his friends prayed to God to be merciful and explain this mystery. God answered and Daniel was able to tell dream and its meaning to the king. What the astrologers thought was impossible was made possible by God through Daniel, a God-fearing man.

The notice to kill all Jewish men, women, and children was posted where they could be seen by everyone all over the kingdom of King Xerxes. Mordecai asked Esther to go to the king and beg him to have pity on her people, the Jews. Initially, Esther thought approaching the king when not invited could cause her death. To her, it was impossible. But Mordecai persevered and reminded Esther to use her privileged position as the queen to beg the king for mercy. Mordecai said,

> "Do not think that because you are in the king's house you alone of all the Jews will escape. [14] For if you remain silent at this time, relief and deliverance for the Jews will arise from another place, but you and your father's family will perish. And who knows but that you have come to your royal position for such a time as this?"

Read Esther 4:9-14. Esther responded by asking all the Jews in Susa to fast: they should not eat or drink for three days, night or day. Mordecai heeded Esther's instructions and days afterwards, what Esther thought was impossible became possible and the order to kill all Jewish men, women, and children was overruled.

Of Lazarus' death, first Martha said to Jesus,

> "*if you had been here, my brother would not have died. But I know that **even now God will give you whatever you ask**.*" - John 11:21-22

Moments later at Lazarus' tomb, Jesus said, "Take away the stone." Now Martha said, "But, Lord, by this time there is a bad odour, for he has been there four days." Does this mean that Martha had given up hope? On Martha's part, it was erosion of confidence and it sometimes happens to Christians too. Martha did not make the later statement days after Jesus had arrived, it was made moments after his arrival. A strong believe that something is possible can suddenly turn into unbelief. But for those who believe in the name of the Son of God, listen to this:

> "*This is the confidence we have in approaching God: that if we ask anything according to his will, he hears us. [15] And if we know that he hears us -whatever we ask- we know that we have what we asked of him.*" - 1 John 5:14-15

There are other examples of things people thought were impossible. Was there an element of doubt in Sanballat and Tobiah regarding the rebuilding of the Walls of Jerusalem or were they just infuriated? If Sanballat and Tobiah were not enraged, then they believed that it was impossible to rebuild the Walls of Jerusalem. They even made a disparaging remark regarding the walls Nehemiah was rebuilding. Look at Nehemiah 4:1-3.

Would the Israelites have preferred to serve the Egyptians than to die in the desert? Read Exodus 14. Were they terrified or they simply thought that crossing the Red Sea was impossible?

Regarding Curses

Have you ever wondered why evil or misfortune befalls someone, a family, a people, or a nation? In some cases, it is the manifestation of an appeal or prayer for evil or misfortune. Before the ten injunctions were given to Moses by God on Mount Sinai, men had standards of what was right or just in behaviour. They also knew there was God and that there were repercussions for unjust behaviour. For example, Joseph likened sleeping with Potiphar's wife to a wicked thing and a sin against God.

This topic provides insight into some of the negative pronouncements (in the form of solemn oaths and curses) by men on others for wrongdoing. As an exercise, and especially for those who may be using this book for bible study, please do the following:

1. Name individuals, a group of people, or a nation that was/were cursed in the scriptures.
2. For the individuals, group of people, or nation you have named, for what reason(s) were they cursed.
3. Was the curse ever removed?
4. Which type of curse will not materialize?
5. Look at curses that were activated or waiting to be activated.

In response to the questions above, let us look at the following subsections:

The Curse for the First Sin

When Adam and Eve ate the forbidden fruit, both of them were cursed.

> "To the woman he said, 'I will make your pains in childbearing very severe; with painful labor you will give birth to children. Your desire will be for your husband, and he will rule over you.'" - Genesis 3:16

> "To Adam he said, 'Because you listened to your wife and ate fruit from the tree about which I commanded you, You must not eat from it. Cursed is the ground because of you; through painful toil you will eat food from it all the days of your life...'" - Genesis 3:1-17

The Curse on Cain

When Cain killed his brother, Abel, the Lord said,

> "...'What have you done? Listen! Your brother's blood cries out to me from the ground. [11] Now you are under a curse and driven from the ground, which opened its mouth to receive your brother's blood from your hand. [12] When you work the ground, it will no longer yield its crops for you. You will be a restless wanderer on the earth.'"
>
> - Genesis 4:1-12

The Curse on Canaan
Noah had three sons named Shem, Ham, and Japheth. Ham being the youngest was the father Canaan. One day, Noah became drunk and lay uncovered inside his tent. Ham saw his father's nakedness and told his brothers what he saw. When Noah awoke from his drunkenness and found out what his youngest son had done to him, he said,

> "Cursed be Canaan! The lowest of slaves will he be to his brothers."
> - Genesis 9:24

The Curse on Reuben, Simeon, and Levi, the Sons of Jacob
In Jacob's last words in Genesis 49:1-28, he pronounced *appropriate* blessing on each of his sons. Noteworthy were the curses on Reuben, Simeon, and Levi. The tongue does have the power of life and death. To Reuben, Jacob's firstborn, he was told, *"Turbulent as the waters, you will no longer excel"* because he slept with his father's concubine, Bilhah (Genesis 35:22).

Simeon and Levi attacked an unsuspecting city with their swords, killing every male. For this reason, Jacob said, "Cursed be their anger, so fierce, and their fury, so cruel! I will scatter them in Jacob and disperse them in Israel." Simeon's and Levi's action caused Jacob to move from the land of the Hivites for fear of attack from the Canaanites and Perizzites.

In the blessing that Moses the man of God pronounced on the

Israelites before his death, the curse on Reuben was 'removed'. He said,

> "Let Reuben live and not die, nor his people be few."
> - Deuteronomy 33:6

On how long curses can run for, especially that of Reuben, consider these three factors:
- Joseph died at the age of 110. Jacob, his father, lived for seventeen years in Egypt.
- A new king, to whom Joseph meant nothing, came to power in Egypt.
- Moses was eighty years old and Aaron eighty-three when they spoke to Pharaoh. Moses, a descendant of Levi, was 120 years old when he died.

Christians must be aware that curses can run for decades in a family or tribe, long after the perpetrator has died. Curses can also be overturned when you stand with God.

Regarding Simeon, he was not mentioned in Moses' blessing on the Israelites in Deuteronomy 33 but was amongst the tribe chosen to stand on Mount Gerizim to bless the people after crossing the Jordan. On the contrary, Levi's foes were cursed and his skills were blessed by Moses (Deuteronomy 33:8-11). The Levites were not scattered but were rewarded with priesthood by the Lord. How did this happen, you may wonder. All the Levites rallied to Moses after Moses destroyed the golden calf Aaron made for the Israelites to worship.

> "So he stood at the entrance to the camp and said, 'Whoever is for the LORD, come to me.' And all the Levites rallied to him.
> ²⁷ "Then he said to them, 'This is what the LORD, the God of Israel, says: Each man strap a sword to his side. Go back and forth through the camp from one end to the other, each killing his brother and friend and neighbour.' ²⁸ The Levites did as Moses commanded, and that day about three thousand of the people died. ²⁹ Then Moses said, 'You have been set apart to the LORD today, for you were against your own sons and brothers, and he has blessed you this day.'" - Exodus 32:26-29.

The Gibeonites were cursed by Joshua.
When the people of Gibeon heard about what Joshua had done to Jericho and Ai, they decided to mislead Joshua and the Israelites. They pretended to come from a very distant country, but they were actually the Israelites' neighbour. To perfect their ruse (that they had been on a very long journey), they presented dry and mouldy loaves of bread, and they wore clothes and sandals that were worn.

> "Joshua made a treaty of peace with them to let them live, and the leaders of the assembly ratified it by oath... Three days after they

made the treaty with the Gibeonites, the Israelites heard that they were neighbours, living near them. ...Then Joshua summoned the Gibeonites and said, 'Why did you deceive us by saying, We live a long way from you, while actually you live near us? ²³ You are now under a curse: You will never be released from service as woodcutters and water carriers for the house of my God.' ...And that is what they are to this day." - Joshua 9:1-23

But the scripture did warn in Leviticus 19:11:

"Do not steal. Do not lie. Do not deceive one another."

The Curse on Gehazi

Thinking that his master was too easy on Naaman, the General whom Elisha healed of leprosy, Gehazi sneaked away to demand gifts from Naaman. When Gehazi returned,

"...Elisha asked him, 'Where have you been, Gehazi?' 'Your servant didn't go anywhere,' Gehazi answered. ²⁶ But Elisha said to him, 'Was not my spirit with you when the man got down from his chariot to meet you? Is this the time to take money or to accept clothes - or olive groves and vineyards, or flocks and herds, or male and female slaves? ²⁷ Naaman's leprosy will cling to you and to your descendants forever.' Then Gehazi went from Elisha's presence and his skin was leprous - it had become as white as snow."

- 2 Kings 5:25-27

The Curse on the Boys Who Jeered at Elisha

Just as Gehazi became leprous in an instant in the example directly above, two bears came out of the woods and mauled forty-two of the boys who said to Elisha, *"Get out of here, baldy!"* Read 2 Kings 2:23-25.

Did Jacob indirectly curse Rachel?

When Laban accused Jacob of stealing his gods, Jacob answered saying "...But if you find anyone who has your gods, that person shall not live" (Genesis 31:31-32). Jacob was a man of integrity, but it was unknown to Jacob that Rachel had stolen the gods. Shortly after returning to Bethel, Rachel died after Benjamin was born. If Jacob's curse was intended for whoever stole Laban's gods, then Jacob's curse worked on Rachel, whom he loved. Do you agree?

If something in your household is missing and you pronounce a curse thinking it was a maid, a driver, a nephew, a niece, a workman, or a lodger who stole it, be warned. Your own child may have done it. Don't alter the destiny of your children.

> "With the tongue we praise our Lord and Father, and with it we curse human beings, who have been made in God's likeness. [10] Out of the same mouth come praise and cursing. My brothers and sisters, this should not be." - James 3:9-10

There are also curses waiting to be activated.

If the people said "Amen" to all the twelve curses in Deuteronomy 27:9-26, do not do any of the things prohibited therein.

Only a causeless curse will not be effective.

The Lord revoked Balaam's curse as you would read in Deuteronomy 23:5:

> "However, the LORD your God would not listen to Balaam but turned the curse into a blessing for you, because the LORD your God loves you."

Balak wanted Balaam to curse the Israelites because *they were too powerful for him.* Also read Numbers 22:6 and Proverbs 26:2.

Concerning Spiritual Gifts

Quite a number of people have succeeded because they diligently used the spiritual gifts they possessed in God's service and in the service of their nations. Biblical examples of such people include Joseph, Joshua, Nehemiah, Bezalel, Daniel, Deborah, and Solomon. But there are various things believers want to know about spiritual gifts, and to fully understand this subject, a set of questions is raised. Let us also bear in mind that since we are created in God's image, all individuals may have certain abilities, found in Christ, which can be of benefit to themselves and other people. Christ said in John 14:12:

> "Very truly I tell you, whoever believes in me will do the works I have been doing, and they will do even greater things than these, because I am going to the Father."

Talents and acquirable skills should not be confused with spiritual gifts. For example, you can train to be a boxer or a swimmer, but you cannot train to be a prophet or a dreamer.

What is the source of spiritual gifts?

A close look at Colossians 1:9 reveals that God is the source of all spiritual gifts.

CONCERNING SPIRITUAL GIFTS | 33

How many spiritual gifts are there? For each spiritual gift you have listed, name at least one person in the bible who possessed it.

For insight, read 1 Corinthians 12, Ephesians 4:11-13, and Romans 12:6-8.

- **Wisdom** - Daniel, Solomon, Bezalel, and Oholiab (Exodus 31:1-7)
- **Singing** - Kenaniah (1 Chronicles 15:22)
- **Dream** - Joseph and Daniel
- **Knowledge** - David, Daniel, and Solomon (2 Chronicles 1:10)
- **Faith** - Read Matthew 14:31, Matthew 8:10, and 2 Timothy 1:5.
- **Prophecy** - Isaiah, Elisha, Elijah, and Jeremiah
- **Healings** - Abraham (Genesis 20:17), Elisha (2 Kings 5), Peter (Acts 3, Acts 4), Paul (Acts 14:9, Acts 28:8), and Mark 6:4-13
- **Working of miracles** - Elijah, Elisha, The Twelve Apostles, and Stephen
- **Speaking in tongues** - Read Acts 2:1-4 and Acts 10:45-47.
- **Interpretation of tongues**
- **Discerning of spirits** - Acts 5:1-3
- **Apostleship** - Read Acts 2:1-4 and Acts 10:45-47.
- **Teaching** - Jesus (Matthew 12:38), Ezra (Ezra 7:6), and Paul (Acts 28:30-31)
- **Evangelism** - Anyone who zealously preached the gospel, so look at Acts 6:4:13, Acts 18:5, and 2 Peter 2:5 (regarding Noah).
- **Administration** - Nehemiah and Joseph
- **Leadership** - Moses, Joshua (Numbers 27:18), and Hezekiah
- **Giving** - Tabitha (Acts 9:36-40) and Cornelius (Acts 10)

- **Mercy** - David (1 Samuel 30:21-25) and Nehemiah (Nehemiah 5)
- **Hospitality** - The Shunammite woman (2 Kings 4:8-10) and Lydia (Acts 16:11-15, 40)
- **Exhortation** - John (Luke 3:18 and Philippians 4:3-5)

How did each named person above obtain the spiritual gift(s) he or she possessed?

There are different kinds of gifts, but the same Spirit distributes them. The fear of God is key for the impartation of spiritual gifts. When the king ordered that Daniel, Hananiah, Mishael, and Azariah be brought into the king's service, Daniel "resolved not to defile himself with the royal food and wine, and he asked the chief official for permission not to defile himself this way."

> "To these four young men God gave knowledge and understanding of all kinds of literature and learning. And Daniel could understand visions and dreams of all kinds. At the end of the time set by the king to bring them into his service, the chief official presented them to Nebuchadnezzar. [19] The king talked with them, and he found none equal to Daniel, Hananiah, Mishael, and Azariah; so they entered the king's service. [20] In every matter of wisdom and understanding about which the king questioned them, he found them ten times better than all the magicians and enchanters in his whole kingdom." - Daniel 1:17-20

Solomon asked for wisdom and God gave him wisdom and very

great insight, and a breadth of understanding as measureless as the sand on the seashore (1 Kings 3:7-9, 1 Kings 4:29).

With respect to Bezalel and Oholiab,

> "*...the Lord said to Moses, ² 'See, I have chosen Bezalel son of Uri, the son of Hur, of the tribe of Judah, ³ and I have filled him with the Spirit of God, with wisdom, with understanding, with knowledge, and with all kinds of skills ⁴ to make artistic designs for work in gold, silver, and bronze, ⁵ to cut and set stones, to work in wood, and to engage in all kinds of crafts. ... I have appointed Oholiab ... to help him.'" - Exodus 31:1-7*

Our Lord, Jesus Christ, grew in wisdom and stature, and in favour with God and man.

Before people like Jeremiah (Jeremiah 1:5), Isaiah (Isaiah 49:1), and Samuel were born, they were set apart by God as prophets to the nations. Elijah was instructed to anoint Elisha, son of Shaphat from Abel Meholah, to succeed him as prophet (1 Kings 19:16). Samuel had God-fearing parents who heeded the instructions of God before the boy Samuel was born. Like Joshua was to Moses, Elisha was loyal to God and Elijah (2 Kings 2:1-3). It is good to note that most prophets of God are also preachers and teachers. For example, Jonah was a prophet (2 Kings 14:25) and a preacher (Jonah 1:2).

On leadership, "Joshua son of Nun was filled with the spirit of wisdom <u>because Moses had laid his hands on him</u>. So the Israelites listened to him and did what the LORD had commanded Moses." - Deuteronomy 34:9

As the Lord instructed, Samuel anointed David in the presence of his brothers, and from that day on, the Spirit of the Lord came powerfully upon David (1 Samuel 16:13-14). Conversely, the Spirit of the Lord departed from Saul, whom David was to succeed, and an evil spirit from the Lord tormented him. That is to say, God gives as he pleases.

In the scriptures, there were people who genuinely wanted to lead in an effort to restore lost glory and to help the poor and oppressed. One such person is Nehemiah. Nehemiah's prayer to God was answered; he was a cupbearer to the King Artaxerxes, he rebuilt the Walls of Jerusalem, and he later became a governor (Nehemiah 1-5).

The apostles of Christ were chosen to preach the gospel of our Lord (Mark 3:14). Christ also opened their minds to understand the scriptures (Luke 24:45).

What is the maximum number of gifts a person can possess?
There is no maximum because God gives spiritual gift as he pleases. Although Daniel, Hananiah, Mishael, and Azariah

possessed knowledge and understanding of all kinds of literature and learning, Daniel alone was distinguished by his understanding of all kinds of visions and dreams. But Daniel, Hananiah, Mishael, and Azariah ate the same food for ten days when they were to be trained for three years before entering the service of Nebuchadnezzar, king of Babylon.

How many spiritual gifts did Jesus have?
He who distributes spiritual gifts possesses all. You cannot give what you do not have.

How can one obtain a spiritual gift?
- You need to repent and be baptized.
- Be obedient. Psalm 119:100 reads, "I have more understanding than the elders, for I obey your precepts."
- Offer your body as a living sacrifice, holy and pleasing to God (Romans 12:1-3). Only then you will be an instrument for special purposes, made holy and useful to the Master, and prepared to do any good work (2 Timothy 2:20-21).
- Spiritual gifts can be obtained through anointing and by the laying-on of hands.

Make inferences from the following bible references as well: Acts 1:8, Acts 2:36-39, Acts 8:9-17, and Acts 10:44-48(while preaching). Acts 19:1-11 with Acts 8:36-40, Acts 9:10-18, Deuteronomy 34:9, Daniel 1:17, 1 Kings 3:4-9, 1 Samuel 16:13, and Matthew 17:20-21.

How are spiritual gifts used in God's service?

Read Romans 12:3-8 and 1 Peter 4:10.

Think of a flock; it needs feeding, growing, tending, and direction. The body of Christ is similar. Christ's instruction to Peter in John 21:17 says, *"Feed my sheep."*

Can a spiritual gift be misused, underutilized, or prevented from use?

In Amos 2:12, they commanded the prophets not to prophesy. Amaziah also said to Amos,

> *"'Get out, you seer! Go back to the land of Judah. Earn your bread there and do your prophesying there. ¹³ Don't prophesy anymore at Bethel, because this is the king's sanctuary and the temple of the kingdom.'"* - Amos 7:12

The prophet Hananiah made a nation trust in lies (Jeremiah 28).

Jonah did not want to preach in Nineveh (Jonah 1:1-3).

To those who speak lies (on the pulpit and as oracles of the Lord),

> *"You shall not misuse the name of the Lord your God, for the Lord will not hold anyone guiltless who misuses his name."*
>
> - Deuteronomy 5:11

Warning:

> *"...Do not neglect your gift, which was given you through prophecy when the body of elders laid their hands on you..."*
>
> - 1 Timothy 4:13-15

Today, some churches do not allow members to prophesy but encourage speaking in tongues, which no one in their congregation can interpret.

What are the consequences of hindering, misusing, or underutilizing spiritual gifts?

Imagine the anguish of being locked away for three days and three nights in a prison cell. Compare that to three days and three nights in the belly of a fish in utter darkness with seaweed wrapped around your head. When you try to escape a divine mission, you may get a similar treatment to that of Jonah.

It will be more beneficial if you read the following bible verses because they outline consequences of hindering the use of spiritual gifts: Amos 2:13-16, Amos 7:14-17, James 4:17, Jeremiah 14:13-15, and Jeremiah 18:18-22.

How can one benefit from possessing a spiritual gift?
Proverbs 22:29 says,

> *"Do you see someone skilled in their work? They will serve before kings; they will not serve before officials of low rank."*

A similar thing should be expected of those who possess spiritual gifts. Joseph and Daniel used their spiritual gifts in the service of a nation. Joseph's family benefited from his elevation, while at Daniel's request, the king appointed Shadrach, Meshach, and Abednego administrators over the province of Babylon. Meanwhile, Daniel himself remained at the royal court. Nehemiah became governor and his reign was beneficial to many. Samuel, being a prophet, was a judge in Israel and he anointed kings. Elijah and Elisha also stood before kings.

Read Genesis 31:10-12, Genesis 41, Daniel 2:46-49, Deuteronomy 1:15, Ezra 7:10-11 (25), 1 Timothy 5:17-18 (double honour), and 2 Corinthians 9.

Are some of these spiritual gifts available to unbelievers?
What has faith got to do with spiritual gifts?

Demand What Is Yours!

Let us consider these occurrences in the bible:

Caleb asked for the hill country, Hebron, to be given to him (Joshua 14, Deuteronomy 1:34-36, Numbers 14:30, and Numbers 32:10-12).

Bathsheba spoke on behalf of Solomon regarding kingship (1 Kings 1).

The **Shunammite woman** asked for her house and land (2 Kings 8:1-6).

David pursued the raiding party (1 Samuel 30 and 2 Samuel 3:12-15).

1. Looking at each of the characters above, was any of the requests put forward peremptorily [a]? Proverbs 25:15 reads, "Through patience a ruler can be persuaded, and a gentle tongue can break a bone."

2. Was each demand justifiable or legitimate? On making a forceful demand, please read 1 Kings 20. To Ahab king of Israel, Ben-Hadad sent messengers to say, "[3]Your silver and your gold are mine; your loveliest wives and children are mine."

3 Is the demander requesting something promised or taken from him or her?

4 Was there any facilitator in each case? If so, in what way(s) did they contribute?

5 What might have happened if each character did not act in the manner he or she did?

6 What lessons can be learned from each of the characters?

Now that we have discussed all of the above, read Luke 6:27-30. What do you think?

a) **Peremptory** *means insisting on immediate attention or obedience*

Don't Be Sluggish; Act Quickly

There are situations in life when you cannot be slow in acting. One such instance involved Zacchaeus, a wealthy tax collector. There are other examples also worth discussing.

Zacchaeus, a chief tax collector (Luke 19:1-9)
Rebekah, a very beautiful virgin, attended to Abraham's servant (Genesis 24:10-21)
David - ran quickly to the battle line to attack Goliath (1 Samuel 17:41-50)
Abigail - acted quickly to avert danger (1 Samuel 25:14-34, 42)
Hushai - warned David to escape (2 Samuel 17:15-22)
Peter - freed from prison (Acts 12:5-11)

1. What prompted each of the above characters to respond in the manner he or she did?
2. Was there any obstacle before each person?
3. How did each person benefit from his or her action?
4. What would have happened if each of the characters above was slow in acting?
5. In what situations can you ask God to act quickly? Read Psalms 70, 71, 141, and 143.

Integrity

Adherence to moral principles; honesty

Looking through the scriptures, one would notice that quite a number of people had integrity. Some were leaders and some were people who showed exemplary behaviour. Having integrity does not mean that you do no wrong; a person with integrity admits wrongdoing and would not pass the buck.

Jesus Christ was recognized as a man of integrity. Read Mark 12:13-15. Paul also conducted himself with integrity, and he chose trusted people to do things for him. Look at 2 Corinthians 1:12 and 2 Corinthians 8:23. Is Acts 6:1-6 relevant? Jacob (Genesis 31:38-42) and Job were men of integrity. Hilkiah was told not to ask the men supervising the repairs to the temple to keep track of the money spent (2 Kings 22). This was because these men were honest.

Can one acquire or develop integrity?
To answer this question, it is good to look at Job 2:3.

What does integrity do for you?
- It protects. - Psalm 25:21
- With integrity, you walk securely. - Proverbs 10:9
- It guides. - Proverbs 11:3

- It puts you in God's plan. - 1 Kings 9:4 and Psalm 25:21
- It can take you to a position of authority. - Nehemiah 7:1-3

Why are people of integrity perceived as stubborn? Read Job 2:9 and Job 27:5.

How can you maintain integrity?
- Possessing integrity is encouraged. - Titus 2:7
- Look at the prayer of David in Psalm 17.
- Practice what you preach. - Philippians 4:9

How Do I Answer?

On a bible study day on which 'The Power in Praise' was slated to be discussed, the subject suddenly changed when a question was raised. The query posed was in connection to a point in the opening prayer rendered by one of the scholars. It was:

> "Someone sitting near you who observed that you always read the bible asked, **'Why do you always read the bible?'** How would you answer him or her referring to the same bible you are reading?"

As simple as it may seem, your answer and the way it is presented matters. Let us look at seven ideal responses with the appropriate bible quotations.

I like reading the bible because the word of the Lord guides me.
> "How sweet are thy words unto my taste, yea, sweeter than honey to my mouth! Through thy precepts I get understanding; therefore I hate every false way. Thy word is a lamp unto my feet, and a light unto my path." - Psalm 119:103-105 KJV

I read the bible because it instructs. I do this day and night to observe what is written in it so that I may be prosperous. The Lord also promised to be with me everywhere I go.
> "This Book of the Law shall not depart out of thy mouth, but thou shalt meditate therein day and night, that thou mayest observe to

do according to all that is written therein. For then thou shalt make thy way prosperous, and then thou shalt have good success. Have not I commanded thee? Be strong and of a good courage; be not afraid, neither be thou dismayed, for the Lord thy God is with thee whithersoever thou goest." - Joshua 1:8-9 KJV

Reading the bible prepares and equips me to do good works.

"All Scripture is given by inspiration of God and is profitable for doctrine, for reproof, for correction, for instruction in righteousness, that the man of God may be perfect, thoroughly equipped for all good works." - 2 Timothy 3:15-16

When I read the bible, it gives joy to my heart.

"The law of the Lord is perfect, reviving the soul. The statutes of the Lord are trustworthy, making wise the simple. The precepts of the Lord are right, giving joy to the heart. The commands of the Lord are radiant, giving light to the eyes." - Psalm 19:7-8

I want to keep my ways pure.

"How can a young man keep his way pure? By living according to your word." - Psalm 119:9

I am instructed in the bible to read it.

"...devote yourself to the public reading of Scripture, to preaching and to teaching." - 1 Timothy 4:13

And finally, try a sassy answer like this: '**I like to be on top (the head).**'

> "The Lord will make you the head, not the tail. If you pay attention to the commands of the Lord your God that I give you this day and carefully follow them, you will always be at the top, never at the bottom." - Deuteronomy 28:13

Do not miss an opportunity.
There are also guidelines on how to answer questions.

> "Be wise in the way you act towards outsiders; make the most of every opportunity. Let your conversation be always full of grace, seasoned with salt, so that you may know how to answer everyone."
> - Colossians 4:5-6

When Herod the king was troubled upon hearing that the King of the Jews, Christ, was born, he called the people's chief priests and teachers of the law to know his place of birth. They replied to him, pointing to the scripture:

> "In Bethlehem in Judea, they replied, for this is what the prophet has written: 'But you, Bethlehem, in the land of Judah, are by no means least among the rulers of Judah; for out of you will come a ruler who will be the shepherd of my people Israel.'"
> - Matthew 2:5-6

They quoted Micah 5:2 in their above reply to Herod the king. Was Herod convinced? Yes, he was (for self-interest). Otherwise he would not have said, 'As soon as you find him, report to me, so that I too may go and worship him' (Matthew 2:7–8). Therefore, referring to the scriptures to answer questions does help.

Caution: "Don't have anything to do with foolish and stupid arguments, because you know they produce quarrels. And the Lord's servant must not quarrel; instead, he must be kind to everyone, able to teach, not resentful." – 2 Timothy 2:23–24

Also, remember that as a Christian, people are watching you. Therefore, "...keep your head in all situations, endure hardship, do the work of an evangelist, discharge all the duties of your ministry" (2 Timothy 4:5).

Never be ashamed of the Word.
Jesus Christ said:

> *"If anyone is ashamed of me and my words, the Son of Man will be ashamed of him when he comes in his glory and in the glory of the Father and of the holy angels."* - Luke 9:26

Dear reader, how would you answer this question:
   Why do you go to the church?

The Power in Praise

To praise is to proclaim or describe the glorious attributes of God with homage and thanksgiving. Praise is your faith in action; it's a declaration of the wonderful works of God we witness and a making known of his long-ago deeds even before our time. Praise acts like a catalyst; it initiates God's reaction because he is a God so near. The Psalmist declared, 'Great is the Lord and most worthy of praise; his greatness no-one can fathom' (Psalm 145:3). Therefore, only a person who understands the sovereignty of God can praise him. The question then is: Can one separate praise from thanksgiving? Discuss this topic to hear various opinions.

Why do you need to praise the Lord?

If you need reasons why you should praise the Lord, first take a look at Psalm 100:3-5:

> "Know that the Lord is God. It is he who made us, and not we ourselves; ...For the Lord is good and his love endures for ever."

Praise him because he made you, he is good to you and you are alive.

> "It is not the dead who praise the Lord, those who go down to silence; it is we who extol the Lord, both now and for evermore."
>
> - Psalm 115:17-18

Also look at Psalm 88:10 KJV:

> "Wilt thou shew wonders to the dead? Shall the dead arise and praise thee?"

It is also a good thing to praise the Lord (Psalm 147:1) and in the time of prosperity to rejoice. Read these references: Deuteronomy 28:47-48, Ecclesiastes 7:14, and James 5:13. You will notice that the scriptures encourage everyone who is happy to praise the Lord.

You need to worship God joyfully. Psalm 100:2 also confirms this.

Look around you for actions bearing witness to the goodness of God; they are reasons why you should praise God. "He is your praise; he is your God, who performed for you those great and awesome wonders you saw with your own eyes" concludes Deuteronomy 10:21. The Psalmist also said, "Let everything that has breath praise the Lord." (Psalm 150:6).

Look too at the testimonies in Deuteronomy 3:24, The Song of Moses (Exodus 15:1-21), and The Songs of Hannah (1 Samuel 2:1-11). They all acknowledged the power of God.

Pray for the Holy Spirit to move you.
There are times when people will not show gratitude for the

goodness of God and there are times when people will be sad. In both situations, we need the Holy Spirit to move us to praise the Lord. In Psalm 51:15, King David requested motivation from God. He exclaimed:

> "O Lord, open my lips, and my mouth will declare your praise."

How do we praise the Lord?
"Tell of his works with songs of joy." - Psalm 107:15-22
You can praise the Lord with songs of joy, with musical instruments, and with dancing. Examine Psalm 150 then discuss.

Do not be ashamed when praising God.
"I will speak of thy testimonies also before kings, and will not be ashamed." - Psalm 119:46 KJV

How often do you praise God?
As long as you are alive, praising God should be a continuous thing. Look at these two references. Hebrews 13:15 KJV:

> "By him therefore let us offer the sacrifice of praise to God **continually**, that is, the fruit of our lips giving thanks to his name."

and Ephesians 5:19-20:

> "Sing and make music in your heart to the Lord, **always** giving

thanks to God the Father for everything, in the name of our Lord Jesus Christ."

King David praised God seven times a day. With a genuine effort, try to emulate him. You will be surprised at the transformation.

"Seven times a day I praise you for your righteous laws."
- Psalm 119:164

THE POWER IN PRAISE

Various examples exist in the bible to refer to. In the examples below, note how praise is followed by the manifestation of the power of God.

Jehoshaphat Defeats Moab and Ammon - 2 Chronicles 20

Faced with a large army from Edom, Jehoshaphat, the king of Judah, was alarmed, and he sought the help of God. He enquired of the Lord, and he proclaimed a fast for all of Judah. When the masses assembled before God, the Lord encouraged them through Jahaziel, saying:

"Listen, King Jehoshaphat and all who live in Judah and Jerusalem! This is what the Lord says to you: 'Do not be afraid or discouraged because of this vast army. For the battle is not yours, but God's.'"
- 2 Chronicles 20:14-15

On receiving encouragement from the Lord, they praised the Lord *'with a very loud voice'* - 2 Chronicles 20:19. And what do you do when you are oozing with confidence in the Lord? You sing! The king 'appointed men to sing to the Lord and to praise him for the splendour of his holiness as they went out at the head of the army, saying: Give thanks to the Lord, for his love endures for ever.'- 2 Chronicles 20:21

As the Lord said, the battle was not Jehoshaphat's:

> **"As they began to sing and praise**, the Lord set ambushes against the men of Ammon and Moab and Mount Seir who were invading Judah, and they were defeated." - 2 Chronicles 20:21*

The victory was not the only manifestation of the power of praise; they also took spoils that took three days to collect.

> *"And when Jehoshaphat and his people came to take away the spoil of them, they found among them in abundance both riches with the dead bodies, and precious jewels, which they stripped off for themselves, more than they could carry away: and they were three days in gathering of the spoil, it was so much."*
>
> *- 2 Chronicles 20:25*

One might ask why an army would go to war with precious jewels. It is only because God blesses his people in mysterious ways.

There was another thing that happened: The kingdom of Jehoshaphat was at peace. Listen to this:

> "The fear of God came upon all the kingdoms of the countries when they heard how the Lord had fought against the enemies of Israel. And the kingdom of Jehoshaphat was at peace, for his God had given him rest on every side." - 2 Chronicle 20:29-30

When you compare the physical and mental energy, numeric strength, and planning required to sing to what is required to fight a war, what Jehoshaphat and his people got by praising God is incomparable. Although our battles today are not physical, we would do well to pray and praise God when faced with a difficulty of any magnitude. Read Deuteronomy 20:1.

Paul & Silas in Prison - Acts 16:25-40

Paul and Silas were imprisoned for the sake of the Gospel but what they did during their first night in prison revealed the awesome power of God (in praise). Unlike the previous example, here, only two people *'were praying and singing hymns to God'* while other inmates listened to them. God does not work with large numbers. The combined efforts of two men praying and singing hymns to God evoked the power of the Almighty:

> "Suddenly there was such a violent earthquake that the foundations of the prison were shaken. At once all the prison doors flew open, and everybody's chains came loose." - Acts 16:26

As a result, the jailor panicked and he asked, 'Sirs, what must I do to be saved?' So they (Paul and Silas) said:

> "Believe in the Lord Jesus, and you will be saved - you and your household." - Acts 16:31

Two things happened then.

1. Paul and Silas were released by God (first) and then the magistrate released them in the morning not knowing what had happened at midnight.

2. The jailor and his family were baptized and they came to believe in God.

The Fall of Jericho - Joshua 6:1-6 (20)

When a 'great wall' stands between you and a promise, what do you do? You need to emit a *great shout*. The walls of Jericho formed an obstacle before Joshua and the children of Israel. To subdue it, they acted as instructed by God.

> "When the trumpets sounded, the people shouted, and at the sound of the trumpet, when the people gave a loud shout, the wall collapsed; so every man charged straight in, and they took the city."
>
> - Joshua 6:20

Unlike the first example, where Jehoshaphat did not have to fight, in this example, Joshua and his people had to engage in battle (Joshua 6:21). But guess what? They fought a weakened people who were terrified by the might of God. The ways of God are truly mysterious.

Conversely, the foundation of the temple of the Lord was laid with a *great shout*. Read Ezra 3:8-13.

> *"When the builders laid the foundation of the temple of the Lord, the priests in their vestments and with trumpets, and the Levites (the sons of Asaph) with cymbals, took their places to praise the Lord, as prescribed by David king of Israel. ¹¹ With praise and thanksgiving they sang to the Lord: He is good; his love to Israel endures for ever. And all the people gave a great shout of praise to the Lord, because the foundation of the house of the Lord was laid."*
> — Ezra 3:10-11

Jesus raised Lazarus from the dead - John 11:38-44
In this example, Jesus Christ *thanked* God rather than praise him. He gave a reason for doing so.

> *"...Then Jesus looked up and said, 'Father, I thank you that you have heard me. ⁴² I knew that you always hear me, but I said this for the benefit of the people standing here, that they may believe that you sent me.'"* - John 11:41-42

When we praise God for his wonderful works, people listening can also benefit as you can see in the above example and in the example involving Paul and Silas. A testimony in favour of Jesus' wonderful works, when heard, can convert souls to believe in Jesus Christ. Testimony develops faith in others.

Be filled with Spirit.
Singing praises to the Lord will fill you with Spirit. One can infer this from Ephesians 5:15-21.

God is the only one you praise.
Looking at Deuteronomy 10:21, God is your praise. He does not like sharing his glory with anyone. Isaiah 42:8 reads:

> "I am the Lord: that is my name: and my glory will I not give to another, neither my praise to graven images."

We must be careful not to equate men to God. Rather, we must revere them as servants of God because he works through them. Please read Acts 14:8–18. Even Christ in flesh did not accept praise from men (John 5:41) for the wonderful works of his Father in heaven. He did not need man's testimony about man, for he knew what was in a man (John 2:25).

What can happen if you refuse to praise the Lord?
Find out in 2 Chronicles 32:25–26 and Deuteronomy 8:11–20 about what can happen when you do not praise God. King Herod's death, as recorded in Acts 12:18–23, arose because he did

not praise God.

> "On the appointed day Herod, wearing his royal robes, sat on his throne and delivered a public address to the people. [22] They shouted, 'This is the voice of a god, not of a man.' [23] Immediately, because Herod did not give praise to God, an angel of the Lord struck him down, and he was eaten by worms and died." - Acts 12:21-23

On Fasting.

When fasting, have you noticed that singing praises, hymns and spiritual songs gives you relief?

Bad Company Corrupts

'Do not be misled: "Bad company corrupts good character."' - 1 Corinthians 15:33

Do you sometimes wonder why some people who started out right in life become immoral or unlawful? Most often, it is due to the type of people they associate with. Modern people put it down to peer pressure. But where can a young man or woman learn good attributes? Psalm 119:9 asks and answers the question:

> "How can a young man keep his way pure? By living according to your word."

Therefore, the scriptures will be the best guide on this subject, regardless of age.

Christians ought to know that the human nature is corruptible and that the words of God severely warned of the danger inherent in mixing with the wrong crowd. Let us look at God's instruction to the Israelites in Exodus 23:31–33.

> "...Do not let them live in your land or they will cause you to sin against me, because the worship of their gods will certainly be a snare to you." - Exodus 23:33

Now look at Psalm 106:34-40 to see what happened to them when they mingled with those nations and adopted their forbidden customs. Bad company, you will agree, does corrupt. Let us look at some examples in the scriptures.

Eve deceived Adam - Genesis 3:1-19

Adam got to eat of the forbidden fruit because of Eve's influence. When God questioned Adam, he replied thus:

> "...The woman you put here with me - she gave me some fruit from the tree, and I ate it." - Genesis 3:12

Adam's explanation (excuse) did not stop God from punishing him and Eve. Read Genesis 3:14-19.

Lot's daughters slept with him.

How did this happen and what was the outcome? Read Genesis 19:30-38. In this example, alcohol that takes away the understanding of people was a factor. Therefore, do not keep the company of drunkards. Read Hosea 4:11. But Proverbs 3:5 says:

> "Trust in the Lord with all your heart and lean not on your own understanding;"

Thinking that there were no more men around her to father a child except her own father, from her own understanding, the older of the two sisters initiated this idea:

> "One day the older daughter said to the younger, 'Our father is old, and there is no man around here to lie with us, as is the custom all over the earth. Let's get our father to drink wine and then lie with him and preserve our family line through our father.'"
>
> - Genesis 19:31-32

Both sisters became pregnant and:

> "The older daughter had a son, and she named him Moab; he is the father of the Moabites of today. The younger daughter also had a son, and she named him Ben-Ammi; he is the father of the Ammonites of today." - Genesis 19:37-38

Read about how the men of Israel indulged in sexual immorality with Moabite women in Numbers 25. Look also at 1 Kings 11:7. They too sacrificed to their gods. Balak, son of Zippor, king of Moab, also hired Balaam to curse the Israelites (Numbers 22).

Esau's Marriage to the Hittites – Genesis 26:34-35
The question is: What is wrong with the Hittite woman? She's a bad influence according to Esau's mother, Rebekah.

> "Then Rebekah said to Isaac, 'I'm disgusted with living because of these Hittite women. If Jacob takes a wife from among the women

of this land, from Hittite women like these, my life will not be worth living.'" - Genesis 27:46

But Abraham forbade Isaac from marrying the daughters of Canaanites (Genesis 24:3). Also read Deuteronomy 7:3.

King Solomon's Idolatry – 1 Kings 11:1-10, 14.
This example shows clearly why any God-fearing man or woman should avoid bad company. King Solomon who had earlier built a house for the Lord (2 Chronicles 5) fell for foreign women and their idols. But he was warned:

> *"...You must not intermarry with them, because they will surely turn your hearts after their gods."* - 1 Kings 11:2

Indeed, the heart of man can be corrupted and that is why every Christian must pray daily to avoid temptation.
Matthew 6:13 reads:

> *"And lead us not into temptation, but deliver us from the evil one."*

Jezebel's Influence on Ahab - 1 Kings 21:1-19, 25-26.
Probably the first mistake Ahab made was to marry Jezebel. Look at this:

> *"He not only considered it trivial to commit the sins of Jeroboam son of Nebat, but he also married Jezebel, daughter of Ethbaal, king*

> *of the Sidonians, and began to serve Baal and worship him."*
>
> *- 1 Kings 16:31*

Was Ahab ignorant of the might of God? No. Read 1 Kings 20:1–2, 13–20, and 28–29. Ahab wanted Naboth's vineyard but Naboth refused. When Jezebel heard about it, she reminded Ahab of his might as king over Israel, and she promised to give Ahab, her husband, Naboth's vineyard. She wrote a letter to discredit Naboth and consequently he was charged.

> *"Proclaim a day of fasting and seat Naboth in a prominent place among the people. But seat two scoundrels opposite him and have them testify that he has cursed both God and the king. Then take him out and stone him to death." - 1 Kings 21:9-10*

Jezebel was a very crafty woman. She knew that cursing God (which is blasphemy) carries a death penalty and that no one would plead for Naboth. But the Lord detests a lying tongue, hands that shed innocent blood, a heart that devises wicked schemes, feet that are quick to rush into evil, and a false witness who pours out lies... (Proverbs 6:16). Jezebel's action fits all of these interdictions, and for this reason the Lord brought calamity upon Ahab and his family:

> *"...because you have sold yourself to do evil in the eyes of the Lord. 'I am going to bring disaster on you. I will consume your descendants and cut off from Ahab every last male in Israel - slave or free." - 1 Kings 21:20-21*

What lessons can one learn from this example? Apart from not associating with pagans, you must not allow your spouse or a member of your family to usurp your authority. The power of Jezebel's influence is seen in the *letters* she wrote (1 Kings 21:8). Could Ahab have withdrawn the letters? Do not forget that Jezebel incited him by saying, 'Is this how you act as king over Israel?'

Another spouse who influenced her husband was Zeresh, Haman's wife. When Haman was expressing how disgusted he was with Mordecai, Zeresh and Haman's friends who were present suggested an evil plan.

> *"His wife Zeresh and all his friends said to him, 'Have a gallows built, seventy-five feet high, and ask the king in the morning to have Mordecai hanged on it. Then go with the king to the dinner and be happy.' This suggestion delighted Haman, and he had the gallows built."* - Esther 5:14

Perhaps they had forgotten that when the wicked digs a deep pit to trap others, they fall into it themselves (Psalm 7:14-16). Haman was hanged on the gallows built to hang Mordecai (Esther 7:10), and at Esther's request, ten of his sons were hanged as well. But what happened to Zeresh? From what she said in Esther 6:13, should she have encouraged her husband to do evil? Bad company does corrupt.

> "'If it pleases the king,' Esther answered, 'give the Jews in Susa permission to carry out this day's edict tomorrow also, and let Haman's ten sons be hanged on gallows.'
>
> ¹⁴ So the king commanded that this be done. An edict was issued in Susa, and they hanged the ten sons of Haman."- Esther 9:13-14

Intermarriage with Pagans - Ezra 9:1-3, 10-12, Ezra 10, and Joshua 23:12-13

The examples above involving Esau, Solomon, and Ahab clearly showed the influence of the pagan women they married. When it comes to marriage, Christians cannot ignore God's commandments. If you marry a pagan, you and/or your children are likely to worship other gods if your spouse does. If you are thinking of how to escape marrying a pagan, listen to this:

> "I find more bitter than death the woman who is a snare, whose heart is a trap and whose hands are chains. **The man who pleases God will escape her**, but the sinner she will ensnare." - Ecclesiastes 7:26

Korah's Rebellion - Numbers 16

Three audaciously rude men managed to influence 250 well-known community leaders who had been appointed members of the council to rebel against Moses, their leader. Were it not for the intervention of Moses and Aaron, the entire assembly would have been destroyed by God.

> "But Moses and Aaron fell face down and cried out, 'O God, God of the spirits of all mankind, will you be angry with the entire assembly when only one man sins?'" - Numbers 16:22

If you are planning a rebellion in your church or your community, state, or nation, walk away now. Have you considered using diplomacy? Have you prayed about your concerns? Listen to this:

> "Resentment kills a fool, and envy slays the simple." - Job 5:2

Bad Company You Should Not Associate with

The bible instructs, **with reasons**, what characters we should not associate with. These biblical bad apples are the same or similar to the bad characters in our world today. Pick them out in the bible quotations below:

- "I urge you, brothers, to watch out for those who cause divisions and put obstacles in your way that are contrary to the teaching you have learned. Keep away from them. For such people are not serving our Lord Christ, but their own appetites. By smooth talk and flattery they deceive the minds of naive people." - Romans 16:17-18

- "Do not make friends with a hot-tempered man, do not associate with one easily angered, or you may learn his ways and get yourself ensnared." - Proverbs 22:24-25

"In the name of the Lord Jesus Christ, we command you, brothers, to keep away from every brother who is idle and does not live according to the teaching you received from us." - 2 Thessalonians 3:6

- *"A gossip betrays a confidence; so avoid a man who talks too much." - Proverbs 20:19*

- *"The accomplice of a thief is his own enemy; he is put under oath and dare not testify." - Proverbs 29:24*

- *"Warn a divisive person once, and then warn him a second time. After that, have nothing to do with him. You may be sure that such a man is warped and sinful; he is self-condemned." - Titus 3:10-11*

- *"^{19} Listen, my son, and be wise, and keep your heart on the right path. ^{20} Do not join those who drink too much wine or gorge themselves on meat, ^{21} for drunkards and gluttons become poor, and drowsiness clothes them in rags." - Proverbs 23:19-21*

A list of people you should have nothing to do with is also in 2 Timothy 3:1-5.

Considering the above instructions and recommendations, **whose company should one keep?** First, consider what the definition of a friend is: a person whom one knows, likes, and trusts. Then apply good judgement to determine whether you know this person you want to befriend. The question remains, can you trust any of the bad companies called out in the bible quotations above? You can only make a good judgement if you are wise. Therefore, get wisdom. Also note that:

> "A good tree cannot bring forth evil fruit, neither can a corrupt tree bring forth good fruit." - Matthew 7:18.

The company you should keep is one who can help you find strength in God. Read 1 Samuel 23:16.

But Christ ate with the sinners!
If this thought is raging in your mind, *'But Christ ate with the sinners,'* you are not alone. In the question raised by the Pharisees, when they saw him eating with many tax collectors and sinners, they referred to Jesus as teacher and he (Christ) in his 'reply' said, *"It is not the healthy who need a doctor, but the sick."* Therefore, to mix with some of the characters addressed above, you will need to be a person who is trained to teach and/or is equipped to heal. For example, a probation officer who is an officer of a court can supervise offenders placed on probation, assist them, and befriend them.

Christ *is* a teacher and also a doctor, and you too can be like him. He said:

> "I tell you the truth, anyone who has faith in me will do what I have been doing. He will do even greater things than these, because I am going to the Father." - John 14:12

How can you help anyone behaving badly?

Listen to this:

> "But you, dear friends, build yourselves up in your most holy faith and pray in the Holy Spirit.
> 21 Keep yourselves in God's love as you wait for the mercy of our Lord Jesus Christ to bring you to eternal life.
> 22 Be merciful to those who doubt; 23 snatch others from the fire and save them; to others show mercy, mixed with fear - hating even the clothing stained by corrupted flesh." - Jude 1:20-23

Things You Could Do

Take bold steps in stemming out bad examples. Look at how Nehemiah outlawed Sabbath trading in Nehemiah 13:15-22.

Stop corrupt communication and note that children usually learn or pick up bad habits from their parents and guardians.

> "Let no corrupt communication proceed out of your mouth, but that which is good to the use of edifying, that it may minister grace unto the hearers." - Ephesians 4:29

Follow the example of Christ.

> "Follow my example, as I follow the example of Christ."
> - 1 Corinthians 11:1

Vessels unto Honour

"But in a great house there are not only vessels of gold and of silver, but also of wood and of earth; and some to honour, and some to dishonour."

— 2 Timothy 2:20 KJV

The bible quotation above lists four types of vessels: vessels made out of gold, silver, wood, and earth. I have chosen a two-pronged approach to explain this topic: the Test in Fire approach and the Drop from a Height approach, which can also be called the Endurance Test. Let us imagine what would happen to each of these vessels if they were dropped from a height or tried by fire. The results of the Endurance Test are pragmatic and clearly show the suitability or appropriateness of each of the aforementioned vessels. Clay is brittle and metal is strong.

Test in Fire Approach

This is a test to know which of the four vessels will change state (physical condition) by fire. Out of the four, only wood will be destroyed in fire. Vessels made out of silver and gold will not melt below 961°C.

Drop from a Height Approach

Out of the four vessels, those made out of earth or wood can be destroyed when dropped from a height and landing on a hard surface.

Now that we know from the two tests above that 'vessels of wood and of earth' can be destroyed, what are these vessels referring to? In 2 Timothy 2:20, the Great House is the church and the vessels of gold, silver, wood, and earth are the different kinds of people you will find in the church. If Christ said, "I have not come to call the righteous, but sinners" (Mark 2:17), then one would expect to find different kinds of people in a church. But once you have been redeemed, how can you ensure that you will be a good workman?

Perhaps you should look at 2 Peter 3:10–14: All elements on earth will still be tested by fire.

If only good people will enter the Kingdom of God, only good people can truly represent Christ and do his work. Can you have a bad sales representative or one who is not trained to promote your product? No one wishing to succeed will purposely undermine a task. Like new employees, men and women of God are tempted or tried. Only in this way can it be determined if they can endure hardship.

How Paul Endured Hardship

The apostle Paul's example should suffice to explain how a Christian can become a vessel unto honour. The best explanation I have found regarding this subject is in the New Living Translation version of the bible. Look below for the list of ways to behave to become an approved workman. You will see various ways in which you can be tested.

> "*³ We live in such a way that no one will stumble because of us, and no one will find fault with our ministry.*
> *⁴ In everything we do, we show that we are true ministers of God. We patiently endure troubles and hardships and calamities of every kind.*
> *⁵ We have been beaten, been put in prison, faced angry mobs, worked to exhaustion, endured sleepless nights, and gone without food.*
> *⁶ We prove ourselves by our purity, our understanding, our patience, our kindness, by the Holy Spirit within us, and by our sincere love.*
> *⁷ We faithfully preach the truth. God's power is working in us. We use the weapons of righteousness in the right hand for attack and the left hand for defense.*
> *⁸ We serve God whether people honour us or despise us, whether they slander us or praise us. We are honest, but they call us impostors.*
> *⁹ We are ignored, even though we are well known. We live close to death, but we are still alive. We have been beaten, but we have not been killed.*
> *¹⁰ Our hearts ache, but we always have joy. We are poor, but we give spiritual riches to others. We own nothing, and yet we have everything.*" - 2 Corinthians 6:3-10

But how can one behave as prescribed above? Take a look at 2 Peter 1:5-9:

> "For this very reason, make every effort to add to your faith goodness; and to goodness, knowledge; and to knowledge, self-control; and to self-control, perseverance; and to perseverance, godliness; and to godliness, brotherly kindness; and to brotherly kindness, love. For if you possess these qualities in increasing measure, they will keep you from being ineffective and unproductive in your knowledge of our Lord Jesus Christ. But if anyone does not have them, he is short-sighted and blind, and has forgotten that he has been cleansed from his past sins."

Once, as one of four speakers at a symposium, I was surprised to note that one of the other presenters would not get up to speak when the emcee addressed him with a lesser title than he felt he deserved. What is more important, one's message or his title (church rank)? Remember, *"We serve God whether people honour us or despise us."*

Let us look at some good examples. There are childless pastors who continually pray for childless couples to have children. There are *'poor'* men of God who will always pray for members of their congregation to prosper. What they lack does not deter them from praying for others.

Yet there are people who would leave a church because they did not get the desired post, rank, or remuneration. Would you quit should a senior pastor make a discourteous remark about you or your work? Are you a suitable workman? Remember that when you "remove the dross from the silver, and out comes material for the silversmith"- Proverbs 25:4. The dross is removed by fire so get ready for the trial.

Ark of The Covenant

How did this topic become a subject of discussion during bible study? There are some actions of God that are deemed unfair by scholars and people who read about them in the bible. One such action relates to the Ark of the Covenant. Take a look at the incident involving Uzzah:

> "When they came to the threshing-floor of Nacon, Uzzah reached out and took hold of the ark of God, because the oxen stumbled. The Lord's anger burned against Uzzah because of his irreverent act; therefore God struck him down and he died there beside the ark of God." - 2 Samuel 6:6-7

The question often asked is: Why would God kill someone trying to help? There was a reason for the way God acted, but before delving into that let us get some details first.

The Construction of the Ark

God requested a freewill offering and from what he received, God directed skilled men to make a tabernacle and other items, including an ark. This ark became a snare to the enemies of Israel. Read Exodus 25:1–21, Exodus 35:21–29, and Exodus 37:1–16. The presence of the Ark of the Covenant worked in mysterious ways against the foes of Israel. There is no better example to show what can come out of a freewill (voluntary) offering to God.

The Content of the Ark

Read Exodus 40:20 then go to Exodus 25:16 and Exodus 34:1.

> "There was nothing in the ark save the two tables of stone which Moses put there at Horeb, when the Lord made a covenant with the children of Israel when they came out of the land of Egypt."
>
> - 1 King 8:9

See also Deuteronomy 10:5.

Who can touch the ark?

Let us look at a set of instructions and observations.

> "Have Aaron your brother brought to you from among the Israelites, with his sons Nadab and Abihu, Eleazar and Ithamar, so that they may serve me as priests." - Exodus 28:1

Deuteronomy 10:8 also reads:

> "At that time the Lord set apart the tribe of Levi to carry the ark of the covenant of the Lord, to stand before the Lord to minister and to pronounce blessings in his name, as they still do today."

By reading 1 Samuel 6:15, you will observe that only the Levites touched the ark.

> "The Levites took down the ark of the Lord, together with the chest containing the gold objects, and placed them on the large rock. On that day the people of Beth Shemesh offered burnt offerings and made sacrifices to the Lord."

In Abinadab's house, Eleazar was consecrated to guard the ark when it was taken in but different people (not consecrated) guarded the ark when it was taken out. Was this an oversight? Take a look:

> "So the men of Kiriath Jearim came and took up the ark of the Lord. They took it to Abinadab's house on the hill and consecrated **Eleazar** his son to guard the ark of the Lord." - 1 Samuel 7:1

> "They set the ark of God on a new cart and brought it from the house of Abinadab, which was on the hill. **Uzzah and Ahio**, sons of Abinadab, were guiding the new cart with the ark of God on it, and Ahio was walking in front of it." - 2 Samuel 6:3-4

The two verses directly above answer the question about Uzzah's death. Uzzah was not consecrated to touch or guard the ark; hence he was struck dead. King David confirmed this in 1 Chronicles 15:12-13 that

> "...It was because you, the Levites, did not bring it up the first time that the Lord our God broke out in anger against us. We did not inquire of him about how to do it in the prescribed way."

Please note that the Eleazar mentioned in Exodus 28:1 is not the same Eleazar in 1 Samuel 7:1. Read Joshua 24:33.

The Purpose of the Ark

Apart from being a snare to the enemies of Israel, the ark had two primary functions: The Israelites enquired of the Lord wherever it was placed and it was used to search for a resting place for them.

> "Place the cover on top of the ark and put in the ark the Testimony, which I will give you. There, above the cover between the two cherubim that are over the ark of the Testimony, I will meet with you and give you all my commands for the Israelites."
>
> - Exodus 25:21-22

Read Judges 20:27-28 and 1 Chronicles 13:3. Concerning searching for a resting place for Israel, read Numbers 10:33-36.

Before the Lord requested the freewill offering from which the ark was made, in Exodus 23:27-28, he promised to send his terror ahead of the Israelites. That terror was the ark of the God of Israel.

> "I will send my terror ahead of you and throw into confusion every nation you encounter. I will make all your enemies turn their backs and run. ..."

The Mysterious Power of the Ark

- The Jordan parted for Israel - Joshua 3:1-17 and Joshua 4:18. For this reason, the Canaanites were terrified and it was easy for the Israelites to takeover Jericho (Joshua 5:1).

- The ark was used in the fall of Jericho - Joshua 6:1-12. Here, Joshua used his initiative by employing the ark.

- When the ark of God was placed in Dagon's temple, Dagon fell before the ark, not once but twice. - 1 Samuel 5

- Sacrifice is needed to return the ark. "If you return the ark of the God of Israel, do not send it away empty." - 1 Samuel 6

- The ark was brought to Jerusalem (2 Samuel 6) and Uzzah was struck dead for touching it. Here, there was an error.

- The Lord blessed the entire household of Obed-Edom. "The ark of the LORD remained in the house of Obed-Edom the Gittite for three months..." - 2 Samuel 6:9-12

- Michal disliked how King David leapt and danced before the Lord as the ark of the Lord entered the City of David. For this reason, Michal was made barren. - 2 Samuel 6:16-23

- The news of the captured ark caused's death. When Eli was told that the ark of God had been captured, he fell backwards off his chair, broke his neck, and died. - 1 Samuel 4:12-18

- Out of the twelve staffs placed in front of the Testimony by Moses, Aaron's staff budded overnight. Under normal conditions, an almond tree will start fruiting approximately two to three years after planting. Read Numbers 17:1-8.

King David's good intention to build a house for the ark was rewarded by God. Please read 1 Chronicles 17:1-14. If God can reward an intention to do good, he will surely reward good doings.

Two examples relating to the ark of God show how God uses his sovereignty. First, he struck dead Uzzah, who attempted to steady the ark when the oxen carrying it stumbled. Second, he rewarded David, whose intention was to build a house for the ark. Amazing!

> *"Oh, the depth of the riches of the wisdom and knowledge of God! How unsearchable his judgments, and his paths beyond tracing out!"* - Romans 11:33

Taming the Tongue

"We all stumble in many ways. If anyone is never at fault in what he says, he is a perfect man, able to keep his whole body in check." - James 3:2

The tongue, when not controlled, gets man into trouble. That is why the scriptures described the tongue as a fire:

"The tongue also is a fire, a world of evil among the parts of the body. It corrupts the whole person, sets the whole course of his life on fire, and is itself set on fire by hell." - James 3:6

The only sin that will not be forgiven is blasphemy (Matthew 12:31–32), which can be committed in either utterance or writing. If the tongue is described as a fire, then it needs to be controlled because fire does nothing but destroy. The most important step in fire fighting is fire prevention. That is, a fire must be prevented from starting in the first place.

Let us look at what Jesus Christ told the Pharisees in Matthew 12:34-35:

"You brood of vipers, how can you who are evil say anything good? For out of the overflow of the heart the mouth speaks. The good man brings good things out of the good stored up in him, and the evil man brings evil things out of the evil stored up in him."

Therefore, one can conclude that the mouth speaks out the thoughts of the heart. Although a man can sin in thought, he can also sin through his speech. You can sin by being proud in your utterances, by lying, by tale bearing, and by blaspheming.

There are numerous biblical examples of how people got into trouble by not controlling their tongue, from a young man seeking recognition from a king to an officer who made a blasphemous remark.

Pharaoh Replying to Moses

God sent Moses and Aaron to say to Pharaoh, 'Let my people go ...' But Pharaoh's reply was irreverent to God. He said:

> "...Who is the Lord, that I should obey his voice to let Israel go?"
> - Exodus 5:1-3

When Moses and Aaron returned to the Lord, God promised that Pharaoh would see his mighty hand. Apart from Pharaoh's horses, chariots, and horsemen perishing in the sea, Egypt was plagued with blood, frogs, gnats, flies, boils, hail, locusts, and darkness. There was also a plague on livestock and of the firstborns. Read Exodus 7, 8, 9, 10, and 11.

> "Then the Lord said to Moses, 'Now you will see what I will do to Pharaoh: Because of my mighty hand he will let them go; because of my mighty hand he will drive them out of his country.'" - Exodus 6:1

A Boaster Speaking about King Saul's Death

A young man who boasted to David that he killed Saul met with his death. Apart from boasting, he also lied because he did not kill Saul. Read 1 Samuel 31:1-6 and 2 Samuel 1:6-16.

Discuss this: Can you boast without lying?

King David's wife despised his dance

Perhaps Michal's remark to her husband's dancing was made out of jealousy. Look closely; her words include 'disrobing in the sight of the slave girls of his servants.'

> "When David returned home to bless his household, Michal daughter of Saul came out to meet him and said, 'How the king of Israel has distinguished himself today, disrobing in the sight of the slave girls of his servants as any vulgar fellow would.'"
>
> - 2 Samuel 6:20-23

Michal, King Saul's daughter, had no children till the day of her death because of what she said.

The Blasphemous Officer

Concerning Elisha's 'About this time tomorrow' prophecy, which promised plenty,

> "The officer on whose arm the king was leaning said to the man of God, 'Look, even if the Lord should open the floodgates of the

heavens, could this happen?' 'You will see it with your own eyes,' answered Elisha, 'but you will not eat any of it!'" - 2 Kings 7:1-2

Just as the man of God had foretold, the officer saw what was predicted but he died without eating of it. Read 2 King 7:17-20.

King David remembered the bitter curses of Shimei
Take time to read this. Did David kill anyone in Saul's family before this time?

> *"⁵ As King David approached Bahurim, a man from the same clan as Saul's family came out from there. His name was Shimei son of Gera, and he cursed as he came out.*
> *⁶ He pelted David and all the king's officials with stones, though all the troops and the special guard were on David's right and left.*
> *⁷ As he cursed, Shimei said, 'Get out, get out, you man of blood, you scoundrel!*
> *⁸ The Lord has repaid you for all the blood you shed in the household of Saul, in whose place you have reigned. The Lord has handed the kingdom over to your son Absalom. You have come to ruin because you are a man of blood!'"* - 2 Samuel 16:5-8 (9-12)

Before David died, he charged Solomon not to consider Shimei innocent. The young king obeyed his father's instruction. Take a look at what Shimei said when Solomon called him.

> *"³⁶ Then the king sent for Shimei and said to him, 'Build yourself a house in Jerusalem and live there, but do not go anywhere else.*

> ³⁷ *The day you leave and cross the Kidron Valley, you can be sure you will die; your blood will be on your own head.'*
> ³⁸ *Shimei answered the king,* ***'What you say is good.*** *Your servant will do as my lord the king has said.' And Shimei stayed in Jerusalem for a long time."* - 1 Kings 2:36-38

Shimei's answer above to King Solomon's order was used against him when he violated the confinement. Please read 1 Kings 2:36-46. Shimei's utterances got him into trouble twice. Instead of saying *'What you say is good'*, could he not have apologised?

This example shows why we should not curse anyone in authority. If they do not act immediately, it does not mean that the offence is forgotten or that we were considered innocent. Also, be careful of brief and casual comments you make about people in high places. Those listening in may inform them as a way to score points. Guard your mouth and listen to this:

> "Curse not the king, no not in thy thought; and curse not the rich in thy bedchamber: for a bird of the air shall carry the voice, and that which hath wings shall tell the matter."
>
> - Ecclesiastes 10:20 KJV

Christ Insulted

This is an example of good and bad speeches. One of the

malefactors hanged alongside Jesus insulted him and the other rebuked the criminal for insulting Christ.

> "³⁹ One of the criminals who hung there hurled insults at him: Aren't you the Christ? Save yourself and us!
> ⁴⁰ But the other criminal rebuked him. 'Don't you fear God,' he said, 'since you are under the same sentence?
> ⁴¹ We are punished justly, for we are getting what our deeds deserve. But this man has done nothing wrong.'
> ⁴² Then he said, 'Jesus, remember me when you come into your kingdom.'
> ⁴³ Jesus answered him, 'I tell you the truth, today you will be with me in paradise.'" - Luke 23:39-43

Zedekiah slapped Micaiah, the prophet

If you are a fake prophet, you do not need to slap a real prophet when he speaks the genuine message of God. And remember this:

> "Do not touch my anointed ones; do my prophets no harm."
>
> - Psalm 105:15

Why was Zedekiah so intensely angered? Examine these prophecies: To the two kings inquiring from God, Zedekiah, who had made iron horns to impress, said,

> "...This is what the Lord says: 'With these you will gore the Arameans until they are destroyed.'" - 1 Kings 22:11

But Micaiah prophesied thus:

> "¹⁹ ... *Finally, a spirit came forward, stood before the Lord and said, 'I will entice him.'*
> ²² *'By what means?' the Lord asked. 'I will go out and be a lying spirit in the mouths of all his prophets,' he said. 'You will succeed in enticing him,' said the Lord. 'Go and do it.'*
> ²³ *So now the Lord has put a lying spirit in the mouths of all these prophets of yours. The Lord has decreed disaster for you.*
> ²⁴ *Then Zedekiah son of Kenaanah went up and slapped Micaiah in the face. 'Which way did the spirit from the Lord go when he went from me to speak to you? he asked.'"* - 1 Kings 22:19-24

Nabal on David

Words calmly spoken can soothe but when you speak harshly, it can enrage and even start strife. David sent men to Nabal with polite greeting but Nabal's reply was so belittling that it enraged David. He said,

> "*...Who is this David? Who is this son of Jesse? Many servants are breaking away from their masters these days.*" - 1 Samuel 25:10

Nabal was later found dead. Read 1 Samuel 25:1-38.
From the eight examples above, you can see that they all reaped the consequences of what they said. Therefore, understand that:

"The tongue has the power of life and death" - Proverbs 18:21

Before God, don't justify yourself

Even when you are blameless, you cannot justify yourself before God. Job justified himself (Job 31) and God replied to him in Job 38. Before he started complaining, look at what Job predicted in Job 9:19-20:

> *"If it is a matter of strength, he is mighty! And if it is a matter of justice, who will summon him? Even if I were innocent,* **my mouth would condemn me***; if I were blameless, it would pronounce me guilty."*

Refrain from Cursing

The tongue can also be used to invoke evil or misfortune upon a person or people. Should a Christian curse? I would say no; for I have seen congregations dwindle, marriages break up, and children become vagabonds because of curses. For these reasons, the scriptures warned:

> " [9] *With the tongue we praise our Lord and Father, and with it we curse men, who have been made in God's likeness.* [10] *Out of the same mouth come praise and cursing. My brothers, this should not be."*
>
> - James 3:9-10

Most importantly, men and women of God must understand that with their anointing comes authority to bless and curse. Why would Balak hire Balaam to curse the Israelites if he knew it would not work? Listen to this:

> "Now come and put a curse on these people, because they are too powerful for me. Perhaps then I will be able to defeat them and drive them out of the country. For I know that those you bless are blessed, and those you curse are cursed." - Numbers 22:6

Parents should also know that they can shape the future of their children with blessing and curses. With his mouth, Noah shaped the future of Ham, Japheth, and Shem. Take a look at this:

> "Ham, the father of Canaan, saw his father's nakedness and told his two brothers outside... When Noah awoke from his wine and found out what his youngest son had done to him, [25] he said, 'Cursed be Canaan! The lowest of slaves will he be to his brothers.' [26] He also said, 'Blessed be the Lord, the God of Shem! May Canaan be the slave of Shem. [27] May God extend the territory of Japheth; may Japheth live in the tents of Shem, and may Canaan be his slave.'" - Genesis 9:22-27

Clearly, Noah was angry when he found out what Ham did. Instead of cursing, surely scolding would have been better. Even before the curse began to manifest, Ham would have been downhearted and probably jealous because his brothers were blessed. For a minute, think of the psychological effect cursing would have on a young man or woman. Like Noah, many parents have pronounced curses on their children. Some children know it and some don't. For those who don't know, that curse stays with them for the rest of their life unless it is spiritually discerned and reversed. Since it is quicker to destroy than to build, curses manifest more quickly than blessing and they can alter the good future destined for a person.

When Rachel, Jacob's wife, stole her father's household gods (Genesis 31:19), it was Jacob who placed a curse on the thief, not Laban, Rachel's father. Again, it was done out of annoyance. Jacob said:

> *"'But if you find anyone who has your gods, he shall not live. In the presence of our relatives, see for yourself whether there is anything of yours here with me; and if so, take it.' Now Jacob did not know that Rachel had stolen the gods."* - Genesis 31:32

Rachel died shortly after giving birth to the baby she was carrying when she stole her father's household gods. Jacob's love for Rachel is shown in the way he arranged his family when he was about to meet Esau after a long time. (Jacob was afraid.)

> *"Jacob looked up and there was Esau, coming with his four hundred men; so he divided the children among Leah, Rachel and the two maidservants.*

> ² He put the maidservants and their children in front, Leah and her children next, and **Rachel and Joseph in the rear.**" - Genesis 33:1-2

When you are not sure, don't curse; you only know your own deeds, not others. Whilst trying to exonerate yourself, you may even place a curse on yourself or relations. Therefore, before you curse anyone, think of this covenant:

> "May those who curse you be cursed and those who bless you be blessed." - Genesis 27:29

What can you do to control your tongue?

To control one's utterance, one would need to exercise self-control. Listen to this:

> "Even a fool is thought wise if he keeps silent, and discerning if he holds his tongue." - Proverbs 17:28

Try not to boast; you cannot brag without talking (or writing).

> "This is what the Lord says: 'Let not the wise man boast of his wisdom or the strong man boast of his strength or the rich man boast of his riches,'" - Jeremiah 9:23

Remember this! The infamous luxury liner, the Titanic ship, was said to be unsinkable, yet it sank in the Atlantic Ocean on its maiden voyage on the 15th of April 1912.

Don't speak rashly.

> "He who guards his lips guards his life, but he who speaks rashly will come to ruin." - Proverbs 13:3

And pray like this:

> "Teach me, and I will hold my tongue: and cause me to understand wherein I have erred." - Job 6:24

The tongue can also kill business. Gerald Ratners, the chief executive of a major British jewellery company, Ratners Group, made a speech at the Institute of Directors on April 23, 1991. In that speech, he commented,

> "We also do cut-glass sherry decanters complete with six glasses on a silver-plated tray that your butler can serve you drinks on, all for £4.95. People say, 'How can you sell this for such a low price?' I say, 'Because it's totally crap.'"

Just because he said "it's totally crap," the group closed 330 jewellery stores and axed about 2,500 jobs in Britain and the U.S., all of this after reporting a massive slide amounting to annual losses of £122M. Sixteen years later, in his own words, Ratners said,

> "It says something about our society that people like to list what I lost in monetary terms: a £650,000 salary, £500M wiped off the valuation of my company, and a billion-pound turnover slashed overnight."

Before you talk, weigh your words.

> "Does not the ear test words as the tongue tastes food?" - Job 12:11

Keeping Plans to Yourself.

It is always good to keep your plan or progress to yourself until it is necessary to reveal it. Why? You may be revealing it to people who may sabotage it. Look at 1 Samuel 10:27 (for troublemakers). When Saul returned from looking for the lost donkeys, he met his uncle but refused to tell him he had been anointed king by Samuel.

> "Now Saul's uncle asked him and his servant, 'Where have you been?' 'Looking for the donkeys,' he said. 'But when we saw they were not to be found, we went to Samuel.' Saul's uncle said, 'Tell me what Samuel said to you.' Saul replied, 'He assured us that the donkeys had been found.' **But he did not tell his uncle what Samuel had said about the kingship.**" - 1 Samuel 10:14-16

Nehemiah also did something similar. He told no one of his plan to rebuild the walls of Jerusalem.

"I set out during the night with a few men. **I had not told anyone what my God had put in my heart to do for Jerusalem.** *There were no mounts with me except the one I was riding on."*

- Nehemiah 2:12

Announce accomplishments not plans. If you are finding it difficult to hold your tongue, use Psalm 141:3 as a prayer:

"Set a guard over my mouth, lord; keep watch over the door of my lips."

What Adversaries Do to Hinder Work

Derived from the books of Ezra & Nehemiah

Good works sometimes have opposition. When the adversaries of the tribes of Judah and Benjamin heard that the twosome were building the temple of the Lord God of Israel, the enemies thought of many schemes they could use to oppose their foes. First, they (the enemies) offered to help. Read Ezra 4:1–3. When this approach did not work, they hired counsellors to frustrate Judah and Benjamin.

> *"Then the peoples around them set out to discourage the people of Judah and make them afraid to go on building. They hired counsellors to work against them and frustrate their plans during the entire reign of Cyrus king of Persia and down to the reign of Darius king of Persia."* - Ezra 4:4-6

The next thing the adversaries did was write a letter of accusation to discredit the inhabitants of Judah and Jerusalem - Ezra 4:7-16 (12-14). However, they succeeded in their third attempt to stop the rebuilding work when the king ordered them to cease work.

WHAT ADVERSARIES DO TO HINDER WORK | 97

> *"'Now issue an order to these men to stop work, so that this city will not be rebuilt until I so order. Be careful not to neglect this matter. Why let this threat grow, to the detriment of the royal interests?' ...Thus the work on the house of God in Jerusalem came to a standstill until the second year of the reign of Darius king of Persia." - Ezra 4:24*

Then the Lord spoke (Ezra 5:1-2) and the rebuilding began with the help of the prophets of God that were with them. Again, the builders were opposed, so their adversaries asked:

> *"...Who authorized you to rebuild this temple and to finish it?"*
> *- Ezra 5:3*

But the builders were bold and 'they were not stopped until a report could go to Darius and his written reply be received.' The governor then wrote to King Darius quoting what the builders said. A vital point in this letter was to see if King Cyrus did in fact issue a decree to rebuild this house of God in Jerusalem (Ezra 5:13-17). Also refer to Ezra 1:1-4. Searches were made on the king's order to find out about the decree. It was discovered to be true and the king issued another decree (Ezra 6:6-12), this one instructing the governor and officials of that province not to interfere with the work on the temple of God. They were also ordered to provide the builders whatever was needed. Ha-ha. Despite the opposition, the builders constructed the temple and finished the job (Ezra 6:13-14).

The lesson here is that even when you have everything you need for a project, you still have to pray against those who can hinder it. Looking at Ezra 2:68-69 and Ezra 3:7, the builders had land, money, manpower, and building materials to build the temple but opposition came in human form. Are you wondering why people were opposed to building a temple for God?

HOW NEHEMIAH SET OUT TO REBUILD THE WALLS OF JERUSALEM

The scripture recommends we commit everything we do to the Lord (Psalm 37:7). To rebuild the ruined walls of Jerusalem, Nehemiah did just that:

- He started by praying to the Lord regarding the project. (See Nehemiah 2:4 ... "So I prayed to the God of heaven.")

- He also sought the king's permission and assistance before setting out. Read Nehemiah 2:6-9.

- He told no one until it was time to execute the plan (rebuilding). There are people who tell all about their plans and they end up achieving nothing.

> "The officials did not know where I had gone or what I was doing, because as yet I had said nothing to the Jews or the priests or nobles or officials or any others who would be doing the work."
>
> - Nehemiah 2:16

THE PLAN OF THE ADVERSARIES

When your plan and the benefits are known to people, opposition may arise and they may want to stop or stall the project or work. In the case of Nehemiah, opposition first came from Sanballat and Tobiah. They even laughed to scorn Nehemiah.

> "When Sanballat the Horonite and Tobiah the Ammonite official heard about this, they were very much disturbed that someone had come to promote the welfare of the Israelites." - Nehemiah 2:10

> "But when Sanballat the Horonite, Tobiah the Ammonite official and Geshem the Arab heard about it, they mocked and ridiculed us. 'What is this you are doing?' they asked. 'Are you rebelling against the king?'" - Nehemiah 2:19

Remind your adversaries about the might of God and answer in a godly manner if you should. Nehemiah's response to Sanballat and Tobiah was godly.

> "I answered them by saying, 'The God of heaven will give us success. We his servants will start rebuilding, but as for you, you have no share in Jerusalem or any claim or historic right to it.'"
> - Nehemiah 2: 20

Once you are sure you are doing the right thing, do not let mocking or criticism put you off a project. Sanballat and Tobiah said,

> "...What they are building - if even a fox climbed up on it, he would break down their wall of stones!" - Nehemiah 4:1-3

Don't give up when you are criticized but do consider constructive criticism that is useful and intended to help or improve your project. People may advise you against setting up a business, selling a product, or acquiring certain skills just because they know that you will prosper from it.

Sanballat and Tobiah tried to falsely accuse Nehemiah of rebellion against the king, but unbeknownst to them, Nehemiah already had the king's approval and assistance regarding the project. "'What are you doing, rebelling against the king like this?' they asked." - Nehemiah 2:19

In a letter sent to Nehemiah, they even accused him of wanting to become king.

> "...It is reported among the nations - and Geshem says it is true - that you and the Jews are plotting to revolt, and therefore you are building the wall. Moreover, according to these reports you are about to become their king..." - Nehemiah 6:6-7

Always make sure your project has the necessary backing of the law.

WHAT ADVERSARIES DO TO HINDER WORK | 101

Sanballat, Tobiah, and Geshem planned to harm Nehemiah.

> "*2 Sanballat and Geshem sent me this message: 'Come, let us meet together in one of the villages on the plain of Ono.' But they were scheming to harm me;*
> *3 so I sent messengers to them with this reply: 'I am carrying on a great project and cannot go down. Why should the work stop while I leave it and go down to you?' 4 Four times they sent me the same message, and each time I gave them the same answer.*"
> — Nehemiah 6:2-4

False prophecy was attempted so as to discredit Nehemiah. Read Nehemiah 6:10-13.

The adversaries did all they could to frighten Nehemiah and the workers but he prayed to God for strength. Listen to this:

> "*For they all made us afraid, saying, 'Their hands shall be weakened from the work, that it be not done.' Now therefore, O God, strengthen my hands.*" - Nehemiah 6:9

HOW NEHEMIAH WORKED TO SUCCEED

When Nehemiah realised that his foes wanted to harm him and his workers, he resorted to this plan: "From that day on, half of my servants worked on construction, and half held the spears, shields, bows, and coats of mail; and the leaders stood behind all the house of Judah, who were building on the wall. Those who carried burdens were laden in such a way that each with one hand laboured on the work and with the other held his weapon." - Nehemiah 4:16 -17

ACCOMPLISHMENT

The rebuilding was completed in fifty-two days. During its dedication, two large choirs performed on the same wall that Sanballat and Tobiah said could not hold a fox.

> "During the dedication of the new wall of Jerusalem ... in the joyous occasion ... I led the leaders of Judah to the top of the wall and organized two large choirs to give thanks. One of the choirs proceeded southward along the top of the wall ... the second choir went northward around the other way to meet them. I followed them, with the other half of the people, along the top of the wall..."
> - Nehemiah 12: 27, 31, 38, 40-43

When God is with you, no matter the size of the opposition, you will succeed. Let us look at Gamaliel's conclusion in Acts 5:38-39.

> "Therefore, in the present case I advise you: Leave these men alone! Let them go! For if their purpose or activity is of human origin, it will fail.
> 39 But if it is from God, you will not be able to stop these men; you will only find yourselves fighting against God."

But remember, what you accomplished wasn't by your might. Therefore, give thanks.

DON'T NEGLECT THE HOUSE OF GOD

Sometimes we live in luxury while the house of God is in ruin. I classify ruin today to be physical, moral, or economical neglect. Some may even ask, 'Why should a church be tastefully decorated?' Don't forget that God instructed Moses to use skilled craftsmen in constructing the tabernacle and the Ark of the Covenant (Exodus 26:1, 31 and Exodus 28:3, 15). Solomon also used skilled craftsmen in the building of the temple (1 King 7:13-14).

Looking at Haggai 1:1-11, God was displeased when his house was left in ruin. He also pointed out that the neglect was why they lacked.

God's Timing

This topic aims to explain how God arranges events to achieve a purpose. To a person who is not spiritual, a series of arranged events is just coincidence (accidental). Some will even say it is a fluke but with God, "There is a time for everything, and a season for every activity under the heavens..." (Ecclesiastes 3:1).

There is more to it though. A wise man once said,

> "I have seen something else under the sun: The race is not to the swift or the battle to the strong, nor does food come to the wise or wealth to the brilliant or favour to the learned; but **time and chance happen to them all.**" - Ecclesiastes 9:11

Two examples in the scriptures clearly show how God arranges events to achieve a purpose.

David versus Goliath

David was not part of the Israelite's army when he defeated Goliath. By chance, he was at the warfront, and at that time, Saul's army needed a saviour. How did David get to the warfront? Here, the key is obedience. He obeyed his father's instruction to take supplies to the front lines. There, David saw an opportunity, a reward for defeating Goliath, and he took it (1 Samuel 17:25). When you compare Goliath's stature to David's, Goliath should have won any encounter between the two of them. But "race is not to the swift or the battle to the strong," and the smaller man won. Also remember: "It is not by sword or spear that the Lord saves; for the battle is the Lord's..." - 1 Samuel 17:47. It is also worth looking at Deuteronomy 7:18 and Deuteronomy 20:1 because God does not use people who are easily terrified for great exploits.

Did Saul deliver Israel from the hand of the Philistines (1 Samuel 9:16) or did God change his mind by anointing David king?

Missing Donkeys

It was not by coincidence that Saul got anointed as king by Samuel; it was the plan of God. In 1 Samuel 9:16, God told Samuel:

> "About this time tomorrow I will send you a man from the land of Benjamin. Anoint him leader over my people Israel; he will deliver my people from the hand of the Philistines. I have looked upon my people, for their cry has reached me."

It began with the missing donkeys (1 Samuel 9:3) and the willingness to do as instructed by a parent. This was followed by the ability to listen to and take advice from a person who was a subordinate. Including the things already mentioned, Saul was also willing and liberal in giving something to the seer (1 Samuel 9:4-10) and this faithfulness brought him before the man of God. In the previous example above, you will notice that David was willing to take a risk to save his people (1 Samuel 17:32) although there was a reward for killing Goliath.

The missing donkeys were found (1 Samuel 9:20 & 1 Samuel 10:2) and searching for them provided a path that took Saul to the man of God, Samuel, who anointed him king as instructed by God. Amazing!

Looking at the two examples cited. All the principles of God's timing have obedience, opportunity/chance, and liberalness associated with them.

Joseph Sent Ahead of His Brothers
Psalm 105:16-22 confirmed that God sent Joseph to Egypt ahead of his family. It was not a coincidence that he did so because the Lord knew that there would be a famine.

> *"He called down famine on the land and destroyed all their supplies of food; and he sent a man before them - Joseph, sold as a slave..."*

Joseph himself confirmed that God sent him to Egypt ahead of his brothers:

> "⁶ For two years now there has been famine in the land, and for the next five years there will not be ploughing and reaping. ⁷ But God sent me ahead of you to preserve for you a remnant on earth and to save your lives by a great deliverance." - Genesis 45:6-7

Joseph showed compassion to the butler and the baker (Genesis 40:5-8) and he also took the opportunity to get out of jail. He said,

> "But when all goes well with you, remember me and show me kindness; mention me to Pharaoh and get me out of this prison."
> - Genesis 40:14

You will notice that Joseph did not ask for any favour from the chief baker; he knew the baker would die (Genesis 40:19). He also requested to be mentioned to Pharaoh, not the prison governor. Pharaoh was the highest in authority in Egypt. Smart move!

Because God was with Joseph, the opportunity came and Joseph took it. He was released when Egypt needed someone discreet and wise. It was just the right time too, because his family was starving as a result of the famine that had struck Egypt and Canaan. Joseph also had a liberal mind; he helped his family.

Fruit of the Spirit

Jesus Christ likened each one of us to a fruit-bearing tree:

> *"A good tree cannot bear bad fruit, and a bad tree cannot bear good fruit. Every tree that does not bear good fruit is cut down and thrown into the fire. Thus, by their fruit you will recognize them."*
>
> *- Matthew 7:18-20*

The scriptures encourage us to live by the Spirit so that we will not please the desires of the sinful nature. To explain this topic, I have designed a short spiritual assessment for which you will need a pencil and eraser. As a suggestion, do not use any writing instrument you cannot erase. For the purpose of the assessment, examine this:

> *"The acts of the sinful nature are obvious: **sexual immorality**, **impurity** and **debauchery**; **idolatry** and **witchcraft**; **hatred**, **discord**, **jealousy**, **fits of rage**, **selfish ambition**, **dissensions**, **factions** and **envy**; **drunkenness**, **orgies**, and the like. I warn you, as I did before, that those who live like this will not inherit the kingdom of God."*
>
> *- Galatians 5:19-21*

Which of the above acts of the sinful nature (the bad fruits) in bold is relevant to you? Please tick the relevant box below if you are so inclined, or you may choose to be discreet.

FRUITS OF THE SPIRIT | 109

Sexual immorality ☐		Impurity	☐
Debauchery ☐		Idolatry	☐
Witchcraft ☐		Hatred	☐
Discord ☐		Jealousy	☐
Fits of rage ☐		Selfish ambition	☐
Dissensions ☐		Factions	☐
Envy ☐		Drunkenness	☐
Orgies ☐			

Are you conscience-stricken? Look again at each of the listed acts above. Which one of them adds value to a human being or the church? Discuss the ill effects of each of them (the physical, financial, and spiritual effects) on any individual indulging in them. It may not be relevant to you but it is worth taking on the next task. If sexual immorality has a physical effect, tick the box under column 'P' next to it; if it has a financial effect, tick the box under column 'F'; and if it has a spiritual effect, tick the box under column 'S'.

	P	F	S		P	F	S
Sexual immorality	☐	☐	☐	Impurity	☐	☐	☐
Debauchery	☐	☐	☐	Idolatry	☐	☐	☐
Witchcraft	☐	☐	☐	Hatred	☐	☐	☐
Discord	☐	☐	☐	Jealousy	☐	☐	☐
Fits of rage	☐	☐	☐	Selfish ambition	☐	☐	☐
Dissensions	☐	☐	☐	Factions	☐	☐	☐
Envy	☐	☐	☐	Drunkenness	☐	☐	☐
Orgies	☐	☐	☐				

Now, let us look at what the fruit of the Spirit should be. With regard to the bible reference directly below, they are the opposite of the acts (bad fruits) listed above:

> *"For the sinful nature desires what is contrary to the Spirit, and the Spirit what is contrary to the sinful nature."* - Galatians 5:17

They are the nine visible qualities of a true Christian life, which is also a physical demonstration of a truly transformed life. From these attributes, you will know if someone is truly a Christian or not. Listen to this:

> *"But the fruit of the Spirit is **love, joy, peace, patience, kindness, goodness, faithfulness, gentleness** and **self-control**. Against such things there is no law."* - Galatians 5:22-23

Now that we have identified the fruit of the Spirit, let us use the last keyword in bold, **self-control**, as a means of preventing the acts of the sinful nature. How many of the acts of the sinful nature can you prevent by exercising self-control? Faintly tick the relevant boxes below. You can discuss this issue in your class, group, or family but apply good judgement.

Sexual immorality	☐	Impurity	☐
Debauchery	☐	Idolatry	☐
Witchcraft	☐	Hatred	☐

Discord	☐	Jealousy	☐
Fits of rage	☐	Selfish ambition	☐
Dissensions	☐	Factions	☐
Envy	☐	Drunkenness	☐
Orgies	☐		

How many of the acts of the sinful nature can you use *joy* to control? Tick the relevant boxes below.

Sexual immorality	☐	Impurity	☐
Debauchery	☐	Idolatry	☐
Witchcraft	☐	Hatred	☐
Discord	☐	Jealousy	☐
Fits of rage	☐	Selfish ambition	☐
Dissensions	☐	Factions	☐
Envy	☐	Drunkenness	☐
Orgies	☐		

How many of the acts of the sinful nature can you use *peace* to control? Tick the relevant boxes below.

Sexual immorality	☐	Impurity	☐
Debauchery	☐	Idolatry	☐
Witchcraft	☐	Hatred	☐
Discord	☐	Jealousy	☐
Fits of rage	☐	Selfish ambition	☐
Dissensions	☐	Factions	☐

Envy ☐   Drunkenness ☐
Orgies ☐

How many of the acts of the sinful nature can you use *patience* to control? Tick the relevant boxes below.

Sexual immorality ☐   Impurity ☐
Debauchery ☐   Idolatry ☐
Witchcraft ☐   Hatred ☐
Discord ☐   Jealousy ☐
Fits of rage ☐   Selfish ambition ☐
Dissensions ☐   Factions ☐
Envy ☐   Drunkenness ☐
Orgies ☐

How many of the acts of the sinful nature can you use *kindness* to control? Tick the relevant boxes below.

Sexual immorality ☐   Impurity ☐
Debauchery ☐   Idolatry ☐
Witchcraft ☐   Hatred ☐
Discord ☐   Jealousy ☐
Fits of rage ☐   Selfish ambition ☐
Dissensions ☐   Factions ☐
Envy ☐   Drunkenness ☐
Orgies ☐

How many of the acts of the sinful nature can you use *goodness* to control? Tick the relevant boxes below.

- Sexual immorality ☐
- Debauchery ☐
- Witchcraft ☐
- Discord ☐
- Fits of rage ☐
- Dissensions ☐
- Envy ☐
- Orgies ☐
- Impurity ☐
- Idolatry ☐
- Hatred ☐
- Jealousy ☐
- Selfish ambition ☐
- Factions ☐
- Drunkenness ☐

How many of the acts of the sinful nature can you use *faithfulness* to control? Tick the relevant boxes below.

- Sexual immorality ☐
- Debauchery ☐
- Witchcraft ☐
- Discord ☐
- Fits of rage ☐
- Dissensions ☐
- Envy ☐
- Orgies ☐
- Impurity ☐
- Idolatry ☐
- Hatred ☐
- Jealousy ☐
- Selfish ambition ☐
- Factions ☐
- Drunkenness ☐

How many of the acts of the sinful nature can you use *gentleness* to control? Tick the relevant boxes below.

Sexual immorality	☐	Impurity	☐
Debauchery	☐	Idolatry	☐
Witchcraft	☐	Hatred	☐
Discord	☐	Jealousy	☐
Fits of rage	☐	Selfish ambition	☐
Dissensions	☐	Factions	☐
Envy	☐	Drunkenness	☐
Orgies	☐		

Lastly, how many of the acts of the sinful nature can you use *love* to control? Tick the relevant boxes below.

Sexual immorality	☐	Impurity	☐
Debauchery	☐	Idolatry	☐
Witchcraft	☐	Hatred	☐
Discord	☐	Jealousy	☐
Fits of rage	☐	Selfish ambition	☐
Dissensions	☐	Factions	☐
Envy	☐	Drunkenness	☐
Orgies	☐		

As a whole, the exercise shows how one can use good to overcome evil. You will agree that to participate in the divine nature and to escape the corruption caused by evil desires, you must:

> "...make every effort to add to your faith goodness; and to goodness, knowledge; and to knowledge, self-control; and to self-control, perseverance; and to perseverance, godliness; and to godliness, brotherly kindness; and to brotherly kindness, love. For if you possess these qualities in increasing measure, they will keep you from being ineffective and unproductive in your knowledge of our Lord Jesus Christ. But if anyone does not have them, he is shortsighted and blind, and has forgotten that he has been cleansed from his past sins." - 2 Peter 1:5-9

The essence of this topic is to reiterate that those who don't live by the Spirit will not inherit the kingdom of God. Everyone needs to possess a good measure of the fruits of the Spirit.

Can you overcome? Try and play **Overcomer**®, a board game I invented based on this chapter. By engaging in a few rounds, you will find out that without the fruit of the Spirit, when you land on the worldly minefields, there is no getting out.

Hezekiah's Achievements and Mistakes

"Hezekiah trusted in the Lord, the God of Israel. There was no one like him among all the kings of Judah, either before him or after him." - 2 Kings 18:5

Perhaps all good Christians would like an uncommon description like the above before and after their death. For Hezekiah, it began by listening to God and obeying his commandments, and anyone wishing to be like him should do the same. The scriptures also said that:

"Hezekiah was successful in everything he did..." - 2 Kings 18:7

See also 2 Chronicles 31:20-21. If Hezekiah succeeded in his endeavours, he must have had a long list of achievements. Although it is not an achievement, he became a king at the age of twenty-five and he trusted in the Lord. He also had the fear of God, which means he was a wise man regardless of his age. Then, 'It is not only the old who are wise, not only the aged who understand what is right.' Read Job 32:6-9 and Job 28:28.

ACHIEVEMENTS

Hezekiah opened the doors of the house of the Lord that were shut and repaired them. Read 2 Chronicles 29:3-11, 36. What happens to a nation when the house of God is neglected? They lack.

> "And in every work that he began in the service of the house of God, and in the law, and in the commandments, to seek his God, he did it with all his heart, and prospered." - 2 Chronicles 31:21

Hezekiah removed the high places and cut down the wooden image. Read 2 Kings 17:7-12 first and then 2 Kings 18:4. The Israelites who attended the Passover went out to the towns of Judah. They smashed the sacred stones and cut down the Asherah poles. - 2 Chronicles 31:1

Hezekiah kept the Passover of the Lord, which had been neglected. - 2 Chronicles 30:1-20

He encouraged those who taught the good knowledge of the Lord. They were so happy and for another seven days they celebrated joyfully. Read 2 Chronicles 30:22-27 and 2 Chronicles 31:2-4.

Just as Moses pleaded with God not to destroy his people, Hezekiah prayed to God to heal the people for attending the Passover without consecrating themselves.

> "Although most of the many people who came from Ephraim, Manasseh, Issachar and Zebulun had not purified themselves, yet they ate the Passover, contrary to what was written. But Hezekiah prayed for them, saying, 'May the Lord, who is good, pardon everyone who sets his heart on seeking God - the Lord, the God of his fathers - even if he is not clean according to the rules of the sanctuary.' And the Lord heard Hezekiah and healed the people."
>
> - 2 Chronicles 30:18-20

People faithfully brought tithes and offerings to the house of God. - 2 Chronicles 31:7-12

Hezekiah built city walls and made weapons and shields in abundance. He organised and encouraged an army. - 2 Chronicles 32:1-8

What about subduing Sennacherib? Surely this action can be counted as an achievement because Sennacherib king of Assyria repeatedly intimidated Hezekiah and his people. Sennacherib's messenger made absurd speeches that insulted the God of Hezekiah (2 Kings 18:21-22). This was enough to weaken the resolve of any strong army. And once an army is filled with fear, their defeat is imminent.

> "This is what the king says: 'Do not let Hezekiah deceive you. He cannot deliver you from my hand.

HEZEKIAH'S ACHIEVEMENTS AND MISTAKES | 119

> ³⁰ Do not let Hezekiah persuade you to trust in the Lord when he says, "The Lord will surely deliver us; this city will not be given into the hand of the king of Assyria."
> ³¹ Do not listen to Hezekiah.' This is what the king of Assyria says: 'Make peace with me and come out to me.'... ³³ Has the god of any nation ever delivered his land from the hand of the king of Assyria?"
> — 2 Kings 18:29-33

When Hezekiah heard of these threats, he acted promptly by praying to God (2 Kings 19:4, 2 Kings 19:14-19) and he requested Isaiah the prophet to pray as well.

> "...Now, O Lord our God, deliver us from his hand, so that all kingdoms on earth may know that you alone, O Lord, are God."
> — 2 Kings 19:14-19

The Lord spoke through Isaiah. He promised victory and that Hezekiah's province would not be invaded by Sennacherib, king of Assyria. Read 2 Kings 9:7, 35-37.

MISTAKES

You may be wondering how someone who was successful in everything he did made mistakes. Did Hezekiah become complacent after years of success? Listen to this:

> "In those days Hezekiah was sick to the death, and prayed unto the

> *Lord: and he spake unto him, and he gave him a sign. But Hezekiah rendered not again according to the benefit done unto him; for his heart was lifted up: therefore there was wrath upon him, and upon Judah and Jerusalem."* - 2 Chronicles 32:24

Notice that he did not thank God for the healing he received.

Hezekiah also showed the Babylonian envoys all that was in his house (2 Kings 20:12-19). For a man who had spent his reign defending his people, it was not the right thing to do. When he was questioned about his action, he had this to say:

> *"Then said Hezekiah unto Isaiah, 'Good is the word of the Lord which thou hast spoken.' And he said, 'Is it not good, if peace and truth be in my days?'"* - 2 Kings 20:19 KJV

What about the days after him? Shouldn't they enjoy peace as well?

Did Hezekiah go against the commandments of God in the two mistakes he made?

The study of the life of Hezekiah teaches quite a number of lessons:
- Wisdom does not come with age.
- It is good when you abhor idol worshipping.

HEZEKIAH'S ACHIEVEMENTS AND MISTAKES | 121

- Be bold when you are faced with challenges.
- Encourage good works and reward the same.
- Don't show-off your wealth.
- Be grateful for whatever the Lord has done for you.
- Above all, trust in the Lord.

Does age have a bearing on leadership? With regard to Solomon, King David said, "My son Solomon, the one whom God has chosen, is young and inexperienced." Nevertheless he prospered and all Israel obeyed him (1 Chronicles 29:1, 23).

Understanding Prophecy

Prophecy is defined as the knowledge of the future revealed by divine source or a prediction uttered under divine inspiration. That is what the dictionary says but this subject has many dimensions to it; may the Lord give us understanding.

Let us not deceive or be deceived. There are three major factors that attract worshippers to a church: the Word, Music, and Prophecy. Don't people want to know what God has 'in stock' for them? I do. Abram did when he was childless and he got a reply from God:

> "² But Abram said, 'O Sovereign Lord, what can you give me since I remain childless and the one who will inherit my estate is Eliezer of Damascus?'
> ³ And Abram said, 'You have given me no children; so a servant in my household will be my heir.'
> ⁴ Then the word of the Lord came to him: 'This man will not be your heir, but a son coming from your own body will be your heir.'"
>
> - Genesis 15:2-4

How does prophecy come?

God gives words and his people see visions. Let us look at the following verses:

UNDERSTANDING PROPHECY

> *"For prophecy never had its origin in the will of man, but men spoke from God as they were carried along by the Holy Spirit."*
>
> *- 2 Peter 1:21*

> *"I spoke to the prophets, gave them many visions and told parables through them."* - Hosea 12:10

> *"...the heavens were opened and I saw visions of God."*
>
> *- Ezekiel 1:1*

The first point to note is that there are other means from which one can find out about the future, but God does not want any Christian to practice witchcraft or use a soothsayer, one who interprets omens, or a sorcerer. Read Deuteronomy 18:9-14. To the Israelites, Moses said,

> *"The Lord your God will raise up for you a prophet like me from among your own brothers. You must listen to him."*
>
> *- Deuteronomy 18:15-19*

But God was mindful of imitation (fake). He said,

> *"But a prophet who presumes to speak in my name anything I have not commanded him to say, or a prophet who speaks in the name of other gods, must be put to death."* - Deuteronomy 18:20

If you are in doubt as to whether a message is from God, listen to this:

> "You may say to yourselves, 'How can we know when a message has not been spoken by the Lord?' If what a prophet proclaims in the name of the Lord does not take place or come true, that is a message the Lord has not spoken. That prophet has spoken presumptuously. Do not be afraid of him."
>
> - Deuteronomy 18:21-22

What about people who are new to prophecy? How can they be cautious of false prophets? Discuss this topic and also look at Deuteronomy 13:1-3.

Can a dream be classified as a prophecy? See Job 33:14-18.

Is prophecy necessary? Looking at Proverbs 29:18 KJV:

> "Where there is no vision, the people perish: but he that keepeth the law, happy is he."

Then one can safely conclude that prophecy is necessary. Examine Amos 8:9-11 and Ezekiel 7:23-27. That prophecy is necessary is evident in the case of King Saul. Read 1 Samuel 28:5-7. He approached a medium when God refused to speak to him (1 Samuel 28:7-9).

Looking at 1 Corinthians 14:3-4 and 12, prophecy strengthens, encourages, and comforts men. It also edifies the church. But some Christians who are lacking experience and understanding disapprove of prophecy for or from their members.

Who can prophesy?

Take a look at this:

> "When they arrived at Gibeah, a procession of prophets met him; the Spirit of God came upon him in power, and he joined in their prophesying. When all those who had formerly known him saw him prophesying with the prophets, they asked each other, 'What is this that has happened to the son of Kish? Is Saul also among the prophets?'" - 1 Samuel 10:10-11 (6)

Eldad and Medad, who were listed among the seventy elders chosen by Moses, prophesied. Read Numbers 11:24-29. As it pleases God, anyone can prophesy. God gave four special people spiritual gifts but he gave one of them understanding in all visions and dreams. Daniel 1:17 reads:

> "As for these four children, God gave them knowledge and skill in all learning and wisdom: and Daniel had understanding in all visions and dreams."

You too can prophesy if it pleases God. This is what to do:

"Follow the way of love and eagerly desire spiritual gifts, especially the gift of prophecy" (1 Corinthians 14:1). But you must remember that "...prophecy never had its origin in the will of man, but men spoke from God as they were carried along by the Holy Spirit" (2 Peter 1:21). Read 1 Corinthians 12:7-11.

Also look at the course of impartation of the Holy Spirit in Acts 8:9-21. Most importantly, when prophesying *your heart must be right with God.*

Why do some men and women of God despise prophecy, a gift from God? They would not allow prophecy in their church.

The various forms of prophecy.
"God may speak in one way or in another." (Job 33:14), therefore, prophecy may come as:

>   **Words of encouragement** - Read 2 Chronicles 15:1-8
>
>   **Condemnation** - Read 1 Samuel 2:27-36 and 1 Kings 14:1-12.
>
>   **Instructions** - Read 1 Samuel 30:5-8, 2 Chronicles 20:14-17, 1 Samuel 10:1-7, and 2 Samuel 24:10-14.
>
>   **A warning** - Read 2 Chronicles 36:15 and 1 Samuel 8:9-18.

A promise - Read 2 Samuel 7:4-17.

A revelation - Read 1 Chronicles 17:1-15.

The plan of God - Refer to Amos 3:1-7.

The name of a child - Read Genesis 17:19, 1 Kings 13:2 and Luke 1:30-31.

Prophecy can even **reveal the heart of man**. Read 1 Samuel 9:18-20 and 1 Corinthians 14:24-25.

Even when you disguise your appearance, God still knows who you are. If God knows who you are, he also knows what you want. Take a look at this:

> "At that time Abijah son of Jeroboam became ill, and Jeroboam said to his wife, 'Go, disguise yourself, so that you won't be recognised as the wife of Jeroboam. Then go to Shiloh. Ahijah the prophet is there - the one who told me I would be king over this people.' ...But the Lord had told Ahijah, 'Jeroboam's wife is coming to ask you about her son, for he is ill, and you are to give her such and such an answer. When she arrives, she will pretend to be someone else.'" - 1 Kings 14:1-5

Positive to Negative

There are times when what we hear from the Lord is good but if one is not careful to obey God, the good news may turn bad. Such an example is the prophecy against the House of Eli. (Read 1 Samuel 2:27-36 and 1 Kings 2:26-27)

> *"'I promised that your house and your father's house would minister before me for ever.' But now the Lord declares: 'Far be it from me! Those who honour me I will honour, but those who despise me will be disdained.'"*

Negative to Positive

Although Hezekiah received a message from God through the prophet Isaiah that he would die, God extended Hezekiah's life when he prayed for mercy. (See 2 Kings 20:1-7.) Why was he able to appease God to change his mind? Read 2 Chronicles 30:21-27 and 2 Chronicles 31:20–21 then look at Psalm 1:1–3. The most important thing here is that Hezekiah prayed to God despite Isaiah's reputation as a good prophet whose prophecy always came to pass. That is, the sender (God) is greater than the messenger (prophet). Therefore, God is not rigid. He can change his mind and you too can pray to him to avert death or any prophecy predicting suffering, injury, or destruction. The people of Nineveh did and Jonah was not pleased. Just make sure that you worship the Lord with all your heart and do not turn your back on him.

Look at 2 Kings 13:14-19. If you were Jehoash, how many times would you have struck the ground? Should he have made frantic efforts in striking the ground several times? Discuss this.

When God Won't Change His Mind
We have seen above that when it pleases God, he changes his mind. But there are instances in the bible where God did not change his mind. Read Isaiah 14:24-27, 2 Kings 10:10-17, and Jeremiah 33:17.

Don't rest on your laurels
Take a look at what Bathsheba and Nathan did concerning Solomon becoming king (1 Kings 1:5-37). 1 Chronicles 22:7-12 confirmed that Solomon would reign, not Adonijah. Even when you know you have a good future ahead, don't just sit and wait for it to come to you. Work at it. If Adonijah got his wish, would Solomon have lived? There are reasons why you should take positive steps.

Some Examples of People and Kings who Benefited from Prophecy
Rebekah went to a seer regarding her pregnancy in Genesis 25:21-24. The seer revealed she was pregnant with twins and that 'the older son will serve your younger son.' Was Rebekah later influenced by this revelation when she told Jacob to stand in the place of Esau to receive their father's blessing? Read Genesis 27.

Saul went to the seer because of the lost donkeys - 1 Samuel 9.

King Uzziah - See 2 Chronicles 26:3-5.

King Hezekiah, regarding Sennacherib's threat, sought the help of God and the prophet Isaiah. Read 2 Chronicles 32:20-23 and 2 Kings 19:1-5 and 20.

King David sought instruction from God when his wives were captured by the Amalekites - 1 Samuel 30:8-20. Read 1 Samuel 22:1-10+, 1 Samuel 23:1-14, and 2 Samuel 2:1-3 for the other issues for which he sought instructions from God.

King Jehoshaphat sought instructions from God when the Moabites and Ammonites, with some of the Meunites, came to make war. Read 2 Chronicles 20:1-3. (He also proclaimed a fast.)

The Danites sought a place of their own through prophecy. - Judges 18:1-6

Can prophecy fail?
Read Ezekiel 12:21-28 first then discuss this question.

What happens when you forbid, hinder, or prevent prophecy?
Read Amos 2:10-12, Amos 7:10-17, and Isaiah 30:8-14 and draw a conclusion. Also, it is not good to mock the prophets of God. As

a result of mocking God's messengers and not doing the will of God, Jerusalem fell to the Babylonians. Read 2 Chronicles 36:15-19.

You should know when you are being deceived

Look at Jeremiah 23:16-17. Sometimes people love to be deceived. See 2 Chronicles 18:1-5, Jeremiah 5:30-31, Jeremiah 7:8-11, and Micah 2:11.

On prophets of deceit, please read Jeremiah 23:30-32 and Ezekiel 13:1-16.

Is there a lying tongue?

Study 1 Kings 22:5-23 and Ezekiel 14:1-11 then discuss this question.

The Last Days. There are two prophecies concerning the last days that are worth looking at. First, Acts 2:16-18 reads:

> "...In the last days, God says, 'I will pour out my Spirit on all people. Your sons and daughters will prophesy, your young men will see visions, your old men will dream dreams...'"

Then 2 Timothy 3:1-7 says,

> "But mark this: There will be terrible times in the last days. People will be lovers of themselves ... having a form of godliness but denying its power..."

These are not fake messages, so one would expect that God will raise more prophets globally.

Music and Prophecy

There seems to be a connection between prophecy and music. Elisha specifically requested that a harpist attend to the king of Israel, Jehoshaphat king of Judah, and the king of Edom. This threesome formed an alliance against the king of Moab, who was rebelling against the king of Israel (2 Kings 3:14-16).

Saul was not a prophet but he prophesied when he met a procession of prophets coming down from the high place playing lyres, tambourines, flutes, and harps. Read 1 Samuel 10:5-11.

King David also set aside singers for the ministry of prophesying.

> "David, together with the commanders of the army, set apart some of the sons of Asaph, Heman and Jeduthun for the **ministry of prophesying**, accompanied by harps, lyres and cymbals..."
>
> - 1 Chronicles 25:1

Men and women of God, take a cue from King David's example and enjoy the gift of God.

Jonah's Expectation

Can anyone hide from the one who knows the heart of man?

"His eyes are on the ways of men; he sees their every step. There is no dark place, no deep shadow, where evildoers can hide."

- Job 34:21-22

The Word of the Lord came to Jonah, saying arise, "Go to the great city of Nineveh and preach against it, because its wickedness has come up before me." (Jonah 1:1-2). Jonah disobeyed the Lord and he fled to Tarshish in a ship.

But there is no hiding place for man when dealing with God, who made the sea and the dry land. A violent storm came to the sea; the ship Jonah was travelling in was likely to be broken. (For he spoke and stirred up a tempest that lifted high the waves - Psalm 107:25). When the waves struck, Jonah was fast asleep. To determine what the cause of their problem was, the shipmen cast lots and the lot fell on Jonah.

Now this is amusing! Before casting lots,

*"All the sailors were afraid and **each cried out to his own god**. And they threw the cargo into the sea to lighten the ship. But Jonah had*

gone below deck, where he lay down and fell into a deep sleep."

- Jonah 1:5

Moments later, the same sailors prayed to God, offered a sacrifice, and made vows to him. This is another proof that idols cannot save; *'they have ears, but cannot hear'*. Jonah said,

> *"Those who cling to worthless idols forfeit the grace that could be theirs." - Jonah 2:8*

This passage shows that if you are repentant, the Lord is ready to forgive. God heard the prayers of the sailors who earlier called on their gods.

Of his own volition, Jonah agreed to be thrown into the sea and the sea calmed down. But the Lord had prepared a fish to swallow up Jonah, and he was in the belly of the fish for three days and three nights (Jonah 1:17). From the belly of the fish, Jonah prayed unto the Lord for deliverance and the Lord heard him.

> *"And the Lord commanded the fish, and it vomited Jonah onto dry land." - Jonah 2:10*

So Jonah was delivered to Nineveh, the place he had earlier refused to go. Does the fish know the great city of Nineveh?

THE MESSAGE

For the second time, the Lord instructed Jonah to go to Nineveh and preach (Jonah 3:2). This time, he went without hesitation, on a three-day journey. "On the first day, Jonah started into the city. He proclaimed: 'Forty more days and Nineveh will be overturned.'" - Jonah 3:4.

The people of Nineveh believed God's message and the king of Nineveh proclaimed a fast throughout the land. Read Jonah 3:5-9.

THE WAY OF THE LORD

"When God saw what they did and how they turned from their evil ways, he had compassion and did not bring upon them the destruction he had threatened." - Jonah 3:10

But our thoughts are not God's thoughts and neither are our ways his ways. His is gracious and compassionate. In Hosea 2:23 he said,

> "...I will show my love to the one I called 'Not my loved one'. I will say to those called 'Not my people', 'You are my people'; and they will say, 'You are my God.'"

God's prophecy to the people through Jonah did not come to pass. Was the message a false one? No. The people of Nineveh heeded the warning and were obedient. Hence, God turned his anger away from them.

THE WAY OF JONAH

God's decision to spare the people of Nineveh displeased Jonah, so he besought God to take his life. Read Jonah 4:1-3.

Still expecting the people of Nineveh to be destroyed, Jonah made a booth outside the city in a place where he could observe what would become of Nineveh.

NINEVEH COMPARED WITH THE GOURD

"And the Lord prepared a gourd, and made it come up over Jonah, that it might be a shadow over his head, to deliver him from his grief. So Jonah was exceedingly glad of the gourd." - Jonah 4:6

The next day, the gourd was destroyed by a worm; there was no shade from the sun, and Jonah "...wished in himself to die, and said, 'It is better for me to die than to live.'" (See Jonah 4:7-9.) Jonah was angry, so the Lord questioned Jonah:

> "...'Do you have a right to be angry about the vine?' 'I do,' he said. 'I am angry enough to die.' But the Lord said, 'You have been concerned about this vine, though you did not tend it or make it grow. It sprang up overnight and died overnight.'"

Jonah was angry at the destruction of a gourd, yet he sat waiting for the destruction of a city with up to 120,000 people.
Today, there are still some Jonahs in churches all over the world.

They are people who eagerly wait for the vision or dream of destruction regarding a person or people in their congregation to come to pass. For a moment, take a look at *'The Watchman's Message'* in Ezekiel 33:10-20. Jonah thought the Lord was not doing the right thing. Don't forget, just like the people of Nineveh, they may be *'people who cannot tell their right hand from their left.'* Therefore, educate them.

Romans 9:15 reads: *"For he says to Moses, 'I will have mercy on whom I have mercy, and I will have compassion on whom I have compassion.'"*

The lessons learned:
- It pays to obey God's instructions. When we don't, we lose the respect he has for us.

- God has control over all beings and nature. He caused the stormy weather, provided a fish whose belly was large enough to contain Jonah, and proffered a gourd to provide him shade.

- God can direct our ways; the fish vomited Jonah on dry land close to Nineveh, where he was sent to preach.

- A message of destruction sent by God through his prophet does not necessarily have to come to pass. Even if the prophet is highly respected and everything he or she says comes to pass, just be repentant and obedient, and don't forget to pray for mercy.

- God is gracious and compassionate.

- Our ways are not God's ways. Listen to this:

  > "...The Lord does not look at the things people look at. People look at the outward appearance, but the Lord looks at the heart."
  > - 1 Samuel 16:7

Jonah had a *second chance*. Will you?

Next time you are thinking of running away from God, remember this:

> "⁷ Where can I go from your Spirit? Where can I flee from your presence?
> ⁸ If I go up to the heavens, you are there; if I make my bed in the depths, you are there." - Psalm 139:7-8

A Scriptural Guide to a Successful Business

Starting a new business can be daunting, and if you already have one, staying ahead of the competition can be unnerving. Get it right and it will look so easy people will want to get on the gravy train. There are principles in the bible that anyone wishing to be successful in business can apply. If these principles worked in the ancient times, they should also work today. Giving your business a name derived from the bible does not guarantee success. It is the business ethics upon which you operate that matter most.

The first step is crucial. Which business do you want to do? If you do not know, seek the guidance of God. Psalm 37:4-5 reads:

> "Delight yourself in the Lord and he will give you the desires of your heart. Commit your way to the Lord; trust in him and he will do this."

Now that you have committed the beginning to the Lord, be patient. Wait for instructions from the Lord. They may come in a dream, they may arise through godly people's advice, or they may come in a prophecy.

> *"To man belong the plans of the heart, but from the Lord comes the reply of the tongue."* - Proverbs 16:1

If you have a strong conviction that what you want to do is the right thing, pray to God to bless your undertaking. You can even lock in a vow. For Jacob, it was a journey; for you, it is a project. Listen to this:

> *"20 Then Jacob made a vow, saying, 'If God will be with me and will watch over me on this journey I am taking and will give me food to eat and clothes to wear 21 so that I return safely to my father's house, then the Lord will be my God 22 and this stone that I have set up as a pillar will be God's house, and of all that you give me I will give you a tenth.'"* - Genesis 28:20-22

There is yet another thing to note: the will of God. This is why you should not force things, rush your plans, or lean on your own understanding. 1 John 5:14 reads:

> *"This is the confidence we have in approaching God: that if we ask anything according to his will, he hears us."*

SET-UP COST

This aspect is very important. What is the set-up cost of the business? This is what Jesus Christ said,

> *"Suppose one of you wants to build a tower. Will he not first sit*

down and estimate the cost to see if he has enough money to complete it?" - Luke 14:28

Therefore, you will need a business plan, a course of action to achieving success that is based on the resources available to you. Even an established business needs a business plan. Take a look at this:

> *"Finish your outdoor work and get your fields ready; after that, build your house."* - Proverbs 24:27

LOCATION

The location of your business matters. If you rely on passing trade, be well advised. If a similar business is already established in the area where you would like your business situated, think of this: *Staying too close could cause rift and stiff competition.* If you are the 'latest kid on the block,' you could be given a run for your money.

Abraham and Lot parted ways because they both had great substance (Genesis 13:5-9). There was also a good distance between Jacob and his boss, Laban.

> *"Then he put a three-day journey between himself and Jacob, while Jacob continued to tend the rest of Laban's flocks."* - Genesis 30:36

SKILLS

Business acumen may be enough to undertake a business that involves buying and selling, but when a business involves special skills, be sure you have the required skill set. If not, employing trained workers may suffice. You can even consider learning the skills that will be useful in running your business.

When Joseph's family came to Egypt to settle, they were presented before Pharaoh as herdsmen. Pharaoh asked if any one of them had the special ability to manage his own livestock. He said to Joseph,

> "...Your father and your brothers have come to you, and the land of Egypt is before you; settle your father and your brothers in the best part of the land. Let them live in Goshen. **And if you know of any among them with special ability, put them in charge of my own livestock.**" - Genesis 47:1-6

When Abram heard that his relative, Lot, had been taken captive, to rescue the captive and because he did not want to fail, he had to use 318 trained servants (Genesis 14:10-14). To build a tabernacle, God instructed Moses to use people filled with wisdom of heart to do all kinds of work (Exodus 35:30-35).

To build the temple of God, David recommended skilful men to Solomon. Their aim was to get the best.

> *"...even they shall be with thee for all the service of the house of God: and there shall be with thee for all manner of workmanship every willing skilful man, for any manner of service..."*
>
> *- 1 Chronicles 28:21*

NOURISH THE BUSINESS

Once you have started trading, don't forget how you started. Just as a seed planted needs water to germinate and the resulting plant needs water to grow, nourish your business with prayer. If you want good success, apply Joshua 1:8. Fasting will also go a long way.

DON'T BE GREEDY

Warning! Your business must not disturb the Sabbath day worship. You should not treasure your business more than your God. The bible warns that Christians must guide against the idols of the heart, for a greedy person is an idolater. Also note that the love of money is the root of all evil.

> *"Put to death, therefore, whatever belongs to your earthly nature: sexual immorality, impurity, lust, evil desires and **greed, which is idolatry**." - Colossians 3:5*

Dishonesty will ruin your business. If you are cheating by charging exorbitant prices, a wealthy person may not be affected if you are selling essential commodities, but what about a poor man buying from you who is struggling to make ends meet? Take a look at this:

> "The Lord abhors dishonest scales, but accurate weights are his delight." - Proverbs 11:1

If you are not convinced, here is a similar verse:

> "Dishonest money dwindles away, but he who gathers money little by little makes it grow." - Proverbs 13:11

SPEND MONEY WISELY

In the bible quotation below, substitute 'choice food and oil' with 'money' and you will get the gist:

> "In the house of the wise are stores of choice food and oil, but a foolish man devours all he has." - Proverbs 21:20

Take a look at this example. Four people who had a lot of experience of making industrial doors teamed up to do business. Before their first sale, that came four months after setting up the business, they leased four cars. Each of them was tied to a three-year lease and there was no sale for four months. The joint business venture ran out of money and they lost their business. Therefore, get your priority right and keep your cost low.

WAGES

You cannot take all the money that the business generates. If you have employees, they must be paid their wages when due (in accordance with your terms). Laban, whom Jacob served for twenty years, did not keep a simple business rule. He changed Jacob's wages ten times (Genesis 31:41). On wages, take a look at these verses:

> *"Do not defraud your neighbour or rob him. Do not hold back the wages of a hired man overnight."* - Leviticus 19:13

> *"Do not take advantage of a hired man who is poor and needy, whether he is a brother Israelite or an alien living in one of your towns.*
> *Pay him his wages each day before sunset, because he is poor and is counting on it. Otherwise he may cry to the Lord against you, and you will be guilty of sin."* - Deuteronomy 24:14-15

> *"Look! The wages you failed to pay the workmen who mowed your fields are crying out against you. The cries of the harvesters have reached the ears of the Lord Almighty."* - James 5:4

TAX AND TITHE

If you are making profit, you will need to pay tax. Recall Matthew 22:17:

> *"...Give to Caesar what is Caesar's, and to God what is God's."*

What is God's? Your tithe and offering. The former is so important that the Lord promises blessing when it is done.

> "'Bring the whole tithe into the storehouse, that there may be food in my house. Test me in this,' says the Lord Almighty, 'and see if I will not throw open the floodgates of heaven and pour out so much blessing that you will not have room enough for it.'" - Malachi 3:10

DON'T FORGET GOD

Now that you are successful, remember how you got there. If you don't, it's at your peril. Deuteronomy 8:8-18 warns:

> "...You may say to yourself, 'My power and the strength of my hands have produced this wealth for me.' But remember the Lord your God, for it is he who gives you the ability to produce wealth..."

There is also advice on stock taking. Proverbs 27:23-27 reads:

> "^{23} Be sure you know the condition of your flocks, give careful attention to your herds; ^{24} for riches do not endure for ever, and a crown is not secure for all generations.
> ^{25} When the hay is removed and new growth appears and the grass from the hills is gathered in, ^{26} the lambs will provide you with clothing, and the goats with the price of a field.
> ^{27} You will have plenty of goats' milk to feed you and your family and to nourish your servant girls."

It is also essential that you know how to apply your success. Be kind and do not oppress.

> "One man gives freely, yet gains even more; another withholds unduly, but comes to poverty. A generous man will prosper; he who refreshes others will himself be refreshed." - Proverbs 11:24-25

REWARD PATRONAGE

If faithfulness is adhering firmly and devotedly to a person or cause, consider rewarding your customers for patronising you. Major superstores all over the world are already doing it. Don't forget that if you are not a monopoly, your customers can buy services or goods elsewhere.

> "The Lord **rewards** every man for his righteousness and *faithfulness*..." - 1 Samuel 26:23

Dealing Wisely

There are two things in life that are of great significance: money and wisdom. Whilst the former is important, people use the latter to stay alive when faced with danger. Wisdom is even used to acquire money. But is the opposite true? Can you use money to acquire wisdom?

Perhaps one should probe further since this topic stimulates discussion anytime it is raised during bible study. Usually in such cases, assertions always arise that it is not justifiable to lie. But is there any gain in acting foolishly when faced with the danger of being killed? When you compare lying to avoid being killed with acting in self-defence to an action that may result in a physical harm-related crime such as assault and battery or homicide, the latter is far weightier. From Abraham to Rahab, there were reasons for dealing wisely to escape death. Did any of their actions (in the examples below) violate morality? Study them with care and conscientiousness.

Take a look at the bible verses that follow.

> "[11] *Wisdom, like an inheritance, is a good thing and benefits those who see the sun.* [12] *Wisdom is a shelter as money is a shelter, but the advantage of knowledge is this: Wisdom preserves those who have it.*" - Ecclesiastes 7:11-12

Let us look at some examples of people who dealt wisely.

Concerning Sarah his wife, Abraham told Abimelech, 'She is my sister' in Genesis 20:1-13.

Ahead of their journey to Egypt even before meeting Abimelech, Abraham foresaw danger and he told Sarah, his wife:

> "...I know what a beautiful woman you are. [12] When the Egyptians see you, they will say, 'This is his wife.' Then they will kill me but will let you live. [13] Say you are my sister, so that I will be treated well for your sake and **my life will be spared** because of you."
>
> - Genesis 12:11-13

Abraham was right in his suspicion because Pharaoh took Sarah as wife. But God intervened, Abraham was reunited with his wife, and Abraham and Sarah were sent on their way. Read Genesis 12:10-20. Abraham also told Abimelech, king of Gerar, what he told Pharaoh's officials: 'She is my sister.' Again, God intervened and Sarah was returned to her husband, Abraham. When you read Genesis 20:1-12, there is a reason for what Abraham did.

> "...There is surely no fear of God in this place, and they will kill me because of my wife." - Genesis 20:11

In Genesis 26:6–10, Isaac lied to the men of Gerar concerning Rebekah, his wife

For the same reason as Abraham, Isaac told the men of Gerar

that his wife, Rebekah, was his sister:

> "When the men of that place asked him about his wife, he said, 'She is my sister,' because he was afraid to say, 'She is my wife.' He thought, 'The men of this place might kill me on account of Rebekah, because she is beautiful.'" - Genesis 26:7

When Abimelech saw Isaac and Rebekah caressing, he summoned Isaac, rebuked him, and gave orders that:

> "...Anyone who molests this man or his wife shall surely be put to death." - Genesis 26:11

Michal, David's wife, tricked her father - 1 Samuel 19

Danger is lurking and you know your husband would be killed if you didn't inform him. What would you do to save him?

When Saul, Michal's father, tried to kill David, this is what she did to save her husband:

> "¹¹ Saul sent men to David's house to watch it and to kill him in the morning. But Michal, David's wife, warned him, 'If you don't run for your life tonight, tomorrow you'll be killed.'
> ¹² So Michal let David down through a window, and he fled and escaped.
> ¹³ Then Michal took an idol and laid it on the bed, covering it with

a garment and putting some goats' hair at the head.
¹⁴ When Saul sent the men to capture David, Michal said, 'He is ill.'"

- 1 Samuel 19:11-14

Concerning Rahab and the Spies - Joshua 2:1-7 and 15-16
When Joshua sent two spies to Jericho, they were lucky to meet Rahab, a woman well-informed about the awesome power of the God of Israel who housed them. She said,

> "We have heard how the Lord dried up the water of the Red Sea for you when you came out of Egypt, and what you did to Sihon and Og, the two kings of the Amorites east of the Jordan, whom you completely destroyed." - Joshua 2:10

But when the king of Jericho heard about the spies, he sent orders to Rahab to bring them out. Rahab did two things:

- Regarding the safety of the spies, she dealt wisely by hiding them and she sent the king's men on a wild goose chase.

- Sensing that Jericho would be conquered, she also took the opportunity to secure the safety of her family, which included her father, mother, brothers and sisters, and their relatives, should the Israelites take the territory.

You can see in the three examples above that the individuals concerned lied so they would not be killed.

Is dealing wisely only about lying to stay alive?

There are situations when people pretend and when they are 'economical with the truth' just to stay alive. These are situations when you cannot consult anyone to advise you on what to do. To save your life, you have to act in an instant.

David feigned insanity. (See 1 Samuel 21:10-15.)

If 'wisdom is better than strength' (Ecclesiastes 9:16), then there is no point fighting your way out of trouble when you can pretend and get away. When David became fearful of Achish king of Gath, he feigned insanity and the king wanted nothing to do with him.

> "¹³ So he feigned insanity in their presence; and while he was in their hands he acted like a madman, making marks on the doors of the gate and letting saliva run down his beard.
> ¹⁴ Achish said to his servants, 'Look at the man! He is insane! Why bring him to me?'" - 1 Samuel 21:13-14

Before David got to Gath, at Nob, he met Ahimelech the priest, and when asked why he (David) was alone:

> "David answered Ahimelech the priest, 'The king charged me with a certain matter and said to me, "No-one is to know anything about your mission and your instructions."'" - 1 Samuel 21:1-2

But David was not on the king's errand; he was on the run because Saul had tried to kill him and one of Saul's servants was with Ahimelech on that day (1 Samuel 21:7). David simply did not want anyone to know he was running away from King Saul. What a way to keep an inquisitive mind quiet.

During the fatal shooting at an island youth camp in Norway in July 2011, one of the victims, Adrian Pracon, dealt wisely. He said he played dead to try to avoid the gunman on Utoeya. Sadly, the death toll was put at 69.

Jacob deceived Laban by not telling him he was running away.
Read Genesis 31:1-2 and 19-21 for the gist of why Jacob was afraid.

Saul dealt wisely with his uncle.
There are times when you should keep information about your progress to yourself. Revealing too much may harm you. When asked, Saul did not tell his uncle what Samuel had said concerning the kingdom.

> "¹⁴ Now Saul's uncle asked him and his servant, 'Where have you been?' 'Looking for the donkeys,' he said. 'But when we saw they were not to be found, we went to Samuel.'
> ¹⁵ Saul's uncle said, 'Tell me what Samuel said to you.'
> ¹⁶ Saul replied, 'He assured us that the donkeys had been found.' But he did not tell his uncle what Samuel had said about the kingship." - 1 Samuel 10:14-16

For what Samuel said regarding the kingdom, please read 1 Samuel 9:20 and 1 Samuel 10:1. Does this mean Saul did not tell the truth? Maybe a look at 1 Samuel 10:27 will convince you that Saul was right to be 'economical with the truth':

> *"But some troublemakers said, 'How can this fellow save us?' They despised him and brought him no gifts."*

The troublemakers may have harmed Saul if they had prior knowledge that he would be made king. Before Saul was crowned king, he was not protected. After he was made king, however, valiant men accompanied him home. Read 1 Samuel 10:26.

Gideon built an altar for God in the night. See Judges 6:25-32. Although Gideon was instructed by God to tear down his father's altar to Baal and to build a proper kind of altar to the Lord, cleverly, he did not do it in the daytime.

> *"So Gideon took ten of his servants and did as the Lord told him. But because he was afraid of his family and the men of the town, he did it at night rather than in the daytime."* - Judges 6:27

When the people carefully investigated, they were told that Gideon did it. As one would expect, they demanded that Gideon must die. But Joash, Gideon's father, met the angry crowd and wisely doused their anger. He made a statement that should the angry crowd act, it would mean Baal was not really a god.

> "³¹ But Joash replied to the hostile crowd around him, 'Are you going to plead Baal's cause? Are you trying to save him? Whoever fights for him shall be put to death by morning! If Baal really is a god, he can defend himself when someone breaks down his altar.'
> ³² So that day they called Gideon Jerub-Baal, saying, 'Let Baal contend with him, because he broke down Baal's altar.'"
>
> - Judges 6:31-32

Samuel applied diplomacy in dealing with God

When carrying out God's instructions, you should apply wisdom wherever or whenever you foresee danger. See below for what Samuel told God when he was sent to anoint David as king while King Saul was still alive.

> "¹ The Lord said to Samuel, 'How long will you mourn for Saul, since I have rejected him as king over Israel? Fill your horn with oil and be on your way; I am sending you to Jesse of Bethlehem. I have chosen one of his sons to be king.'
> ² But Samuel said, **'How can I go? Saul will hear about it and kill me.'** The Lord said, 'Take a heifer with you and say, "I have come to sacrifice to the Lord."'" - 1 Samuel 16:1-2

Was Samuel going to sacrifice or anoint a king? The burdensome task of anointing a new king while another was on the throne was made easy for Samuel. Even with the might of God behind us, we are required to apply wisdom when doing his work. Read 1 Samuel 16:1-5.

Three Devastating Options before David

You are a king faced with three options of punishment from God for the wrong you did. Which one would you choose? Remember you cannot consult and you must answer in an instant. Here are the options:

- Shall there come upon you three years of famine in your land?

- Shall you face three months of fleeing from your enemies while they pursue you?

- Shall you endure three days of plague in your land?

Consider the weight of each of the options. Have you made up your mind? It is a difficult choice to make but let us see what King David did. Cleverly, he did not make a choice; he made only a statement:

> "...I am in deep distress. Let us fall into the hands of the Lord, for his mercy is great; but do not let me fall into the hands of men."
>
> - 2 Samuel 24:14

And God dealt as he pleased. Read 2 Samuel 24:10-17.

When company directors and chief executives place relatives in strategic positions in their companies, are they dealing wisely or is it nepotism? Look at 2 Chronicles 11:21-23 on Rehoboam's strategy.

Joseph dealt on behalf of his brothers. He told them what to say before Pharaoh when they came to Egypt during the famine. They were placed in the best land in Goshen. Please read Genesis 46:31-34 and Genesis 47:1-6. If Joseph did not act the way he did, there was a risk his family would become destitute. Take a look:

> "...This is what your son Joseph says: 'God has made me lord of all Egypt. Come down to me; don't delay.'
> [10] You shall live in the region of Goshen and be near me - you, your children and grandchildren, your flocks and herds, and all you have.
> [11] I will provide for you there, because five years of famine are still to come. Otherwise you and your household and all who belong to you will become destitute.'" - Genesis 45:9-11

True! Psalm 25:12 says, "Who, then, is the man that fears the Lord? He will instruct him in the way chosen for him."

Tamar sought a pledge from her father-in-law; an evidence for the future (Genesis 38).

Put the *sexual act* of both Tamar and Judah aside and think of the bereavement suffered by them. It is easy to pick on what they did wrong and not consider what they both suffered. Judah lost his wife and two sons, Er and Onan, while Tamar lost 'two husbands.' But one thing was on Tamar's mind: She wanted a child fathered by a man from Judah's family. When she heard that Judah had recovered from his grief and was on his way to Timnah:

> "She took off her widow's clothes, covered herself with a veil to disguise herself, and then sat down at the entrance to Enaim, which is on the road to Timnah. For she saw that, though Shelah had now grown up, she had not been given to him as his wife."
>
> - Genesis 38:14

Judah, not realising that she was his daughter-in-law, went over to her by the roadside and said:

> "¹⁶ 'Come now, let me sleep with you.' **'And what will you give me to sleep with you?'** *she asked.*
> ¹⁷ *'I'll send you a young goat from my flock,' he said.* **'Will you give me something as a pledge until you send it?'** *she asked.*
> ¹⁸ *He said, 'What pledge should I give you?'* **Your seal and its cord, and the staff in your hand,'** *she answered. So he gave them to her*

and slept with her, and she became pregnant by him."

- Genesis 38:16-18

When you carefully examine Tamar's questions and answer above in bold, she acted wisely. That is because the seal and cord and staff saved her from being 'burnt alive' as adjudged by Judah (through whom she became pregnant) when she was accused of becoming pregnant by prostitution. Surely you will agree that Judah's seal and cord and staff were more significant than a young goat, and she took the pledge before sleeping with Judah. Therefore, closing a deal properly is important. Never assume a promise to be true.

Jacob was always careful when he dealt; his dealings were sealed with oaths. See Genesis 25:33 and Genesis 31:53.

Daniel interprets a dream then sets up appointments.
No one could interpret King Nebuchadnezzar's dream, so a decree was issued to put the wise men to death, and men were sent to kill Daniel and his friends.

Not only did Daniel stop the execution of all the wise men of Babylon, but he also interpreted the dream. In addition, he requested that Shadrach, Meshach, and Abednego be appointed as administrators over the province of Babylon. Read Daniel 2. His request was well-timed.

Contentment

Contentment can be described as a state of being satisfied with one's present condition or state of being. Because our nature differs, so do areas in which we show discontent. Unless you are spiritually strong, you are likely to whine whenever you want something and cannot get it or when you desire more than you are given. To understand this subject, let us look at aspects of life where people long for what they do not have or for something bigger, better, or costlier than what they currently have.

Areas Where Discontent Is Predominant
- Marriage and relationships
- Physique and beauty
- Material things, food, and money
- Power (administrative, political, and spiritual)

If wealth is abundance of valuable material possessions or resources, then let us look at the futility of wealth in the following bible quotation:

> "Those who love money will never have enough. How meaningless to think that wealth brings true happiness! [11] The more you have, the more people come to help you spend it. So what good is wealth

- except perhaps to watch it slip through your fingers! ¹² *People who work hard sleep well, whether they eat little or much. But the rich seldom get a good night's sleep."* - Ecclesiastes 5:10-12 NLT

Hard Fact

Before we proceed, list the number of prayer requests you have made 'since record began.' How many of them have been answered by God? Considering that Jesus Christ said, 'Ask and it will be given to you' (Matthew 7:7), we should get whatever we desire and ask for. But does it work like that? Take a look at this:

> *"This is the confidence we have in approaching God: that if we ask anything according to his will, he hears us. And if we know that he hears us - whatever we ask - we know that we have what we asked of him."* - 1 John 5:14-15

Looking at the bible quotation directly above, a condition is attached to a prayer request. That is, your prayer will be answered if it is according to the will of God. Therefore, it means we do not always get what we wish for. If you are not convinced, look at 2 Corinthians 12:6-8. Another reason a request may not be granted by God is if you ask with wrong motives.

> *"When you ask, you do not receive, because you ask with wrong motives, that you may spend what you get on your pleasures."*
>
> - James 4:3

But is your life measured by how much money or goods you own? The parable of the Rich Fool in Luke 12:13-21, as told by Jesus Christ, explains this. Consider that you brought nothing to this world and you will carry nothing away (1 Timothy 6:7).

What brings lack of contentment?
- Chief amongst them is greed
- The desire to attract notice and impress others
- Complex (a feeling of inferiority)
- Poverty

Examples Showing Discontent and Contentment.
Israel lusted for meat when God already gave them Manna (bread from heaven). Their action displeased God and Moses. Read Numbers 11:4-7, 18-20, and 31-33. See also Psalm 106:13-15.

Gehazi, thinking his master was too easy on Naaman, lied to receive gifts from him (without his master's consent). Read 2 Kings 5:15-27 and Proverbs 15:27.

Esther asked for nothing except what was suggested by Hegai. This is an example of contentment (Esther 2:15-17). Read 1 Timothy 6:6.

Ahab took possession of Naboth's vineyard by dubious means (1 Kings 21). Although Ahab offered to pay for the vineyard, when

Naboth refused, Jezebel, his wife, rolled out a plan that could not fail. Couldn't the king have put his vegetable garden elsewhere?

How to Be Content
- Learn how to be content, seek Christ's help, and try to differentiate between **need** and **wish**. - Philippians 4:11-13
- Regard pleasures as meaningless. - Ecclesiastes 2:1-11
- Enjoy good times. - Ecclesiastes 7:13-14
- Understand that God chooses whom to show mercy. - Romans 9:13-18
- Don't love money. - Ecclesiastes 5:10, Hebrews 13:5, and 1 Timothy 6:10-11
- Ask for two favours from God. - Proverbs 30:7-9
- Above all, seek first the Kingdom of God. - Matthew 6:30-33

Look at this advice from Christ:

> "'Don't collect any more than you are required to', he told them. Then some soldiers asked him, 'And what should we do?' He replied, 'Don't extort money and don't accuse people falsely - be content with your pay.'" - Luke 3:13-14

Discuss patience under affliction. Is there a conflict between patience and ambition (a strong desire for success, achievement, or distinction)? Note: "The plans of the diligent lead to profit as surely as haste leads to poverty." - Proverbs 21:5

But two questions come to mind that are worth discussing...
Can you aspire even when content?
When does contentment become laziness?

What Lack of Contentment Can Lead You to Do
- Tell lies.

- Oppress or become selfish.

- Be unfaithful to God by consulting fortune-tellers, using sorcery, or engaging in witchcraft to fast-forward blessing.

- Steal, defraud, or do unlawful things like drug trafficking.

- Disfigure yourself through skin bleaching or failed plastic surgery, done to improve self-confidence or reverse the aesthetic signs of aging. However, surgery to correct physical shortcomings and deformities should not be discouraged.

- Cause you to physically harm, defame character, or kill a person whose position or possession you want.

- Displease God.

Opportunity: Sense It & Grab It

A driven person is constantly looking for circumstances that will favour him or her. Sometimes you are even presented with an opportunity without looking for it. Answered prayer may also come in the form of an opportunity. But how can you sense when an opportunity arises and when to grab it?

Let us look at how opportunity comes.

> "I have seen something else under the sun: The race is not to the swift or the battle to the strong, nor does food come to the wise or wealth to the brilliant or favour to the learned; but time and chance happen to them all." - Ecclesiastes 9:11

Regardless of your ability, circumstances that will favour you will come by chance ...by being in the right place at the right time or by saying the right thing at the right time. Here are some examples.

Reward for Killing Goliath
By chance, David arrived at the warfront when the Israelites were saying,

> "...Do you see how this man keeps coming out? He comes out to defy Israel. The king will give great wealth to the man who kills him. He will also give him his daughter in marriage and will exempt his father's family from taxes in Israel." - 1 Samuel 17:25

In 1 Samuel 17:26 and 30, to confirm, David asked the soldiers who were standing nearby about the reward. To David, it was an opportunity because of his ability and confidence in the Lord. Although David was discouraged by Eliab, his oldest brother, he defeated Goliath, a man over nine feet tall. David was at the right place at the right time and he also said the right thing at the right time. Look at this:

> "What David said was overheard and reported to Saul, and Saul sent for him. ³² David said to Saul, 'Let no-one lose heart on account of this Philistine; your servant will go and fight him.'"
>
> - 1 Samuel 17:31-32

When people who do not have the same abilities as you discourage you from taking up a role, business venture, or academic pursuit that you know will be profitable or rewarding, don't be deterred. Eliab thought that David was trying to seem cleverer than the rest of them; the young man was brave, quick-witted, and able to ascertain what he would get before facing Goliath.

Mordecai put forward Esther

To replace Queen Vashti, the king took the advice of his personal attendants and the plan was put into effect. That is:

> *"...Let a search be made for beautiful young virgins for the king... Then let the girl who pleases the king be queen instead of Vashti..."*
> - Esther 2:2-4

You may be wondering where an opportunity lies in the bible quotation above for Mordecai, a Jew in the midst of the Persians. Here is the opportunity: *"a beautiful young virgin to be made queen."* You will notice that no nationality was specified for the beautiful young virgin. Therefore, Mordecai put forward his cousin, Esther, who was lovely in form and features (Esther 2:7-8). Esther, also recognising what could disqualify her, kept quiet about it.

> *"Esther had not revealed her nationality and family background, because Mordecai had forbidden her to do so."* - Esther 2:10

By divine favour, Esther became queen. Rather than disqualify yourself when next you see an opportunity because of the things not asked for, seize it and keep quiet about the qualifications you do not have. As in the above example, an opportunity may not be for you but for someone close to you from which you may or may not benefit.

Joseph and the Butler

The bible did not specify how long Joseph was to spend in prison but an opportunity arose when he interpreted the butler's dream. To be free, Joseph made an earnest request saying,

> "But when all goes well with you, remember me and show me kindness; mention me to Pharaoh and get me out of this prison. [15] For I was forcibly carried off from the land of the Hebrews, and even here I have done nothing to deserve being put in a dungeon."
>
> - Genesis 40:14-15

The opportunity here is meeting an influential person who knows Pharaoh, the king who can order Joseph's release. How did Joseph take the opportunity? He made sure he spoke about his ordeal and mentioned by name the person who could make things happen. He said the right thing at the right time. There are situations or places where you should not be a loner (a person who avoids the company or assistance of others). Apart from good behaviour, Joseph's path to freedom began with this statement: 'Why are your faces so sad today?' Read Genesis 40:7.

Is opportunity about meeting people? Yes. Meeting the butler created an avenue for Joseph to meet Pharaoh. Joseph's ability to interpret dreams was also a factor, and he used it effectively through the help of God when he was called to interpret Pharaoh's dream. Joseph wanted only to be free; he was liberated and appointed the deputy to Pharaoh. Read Genesis 41:9-40.

As it was in those days and today, networking will help you develop and maintain contacts and personal connections with a variety of people who might be helpful to you and your career or business.

Naaman and the Little Maid - 2 Kings 5

Sometimes an opportunity may come from an unlikely source, so never under estimate the recommendation of your maid or the lowly placed. Naaman was the commander of King Aram's army and through him, God gave Aram great victories. But Naaman had leprosy, so his maid said:

> "...If only my master would see the prophet who is in Samaria! He would cure him of his leprosy." - 2 Kings 5:3

Without meeting Elisha face to face and by the persuasion of his officers, Naaman was cured of leprosy when he did as instructed by the man of God. Your breakthrough may come from meeting with a man or woman of God. Had Naaman refused the recommendation of the little maid or if his wife had discounted the servant's words, Naaman would have died a leper.

Saul and the Missing Donkeys.
Just when you are tired of trying, an opportunity may arise.

Having searched thoroughly for the missing donkeys, Saul told his servant,

> "...Come, let's go back, or my father will stop thinking about the donkeys and start worrying about us." - 1 Samuel 9:5

His servant's reply presented an opportunity he almost rejected because he had no money (gift). Listen to this:

> "...Look, in this town there is a man of God; he is highly respected, and everything he says comes true. Let's go there now. Perhaps he will tell us what way to take.
> 7 Saul said to his servant, 'If we go, what can we give the man? The food in our sacks is gone. We have no gift to take to the man of God. What do we have?'" - 1 Samuel 9:6-7

Would you feel too big to take money offered to you by your subordinate or servant should the need arise? Saul's servant persuaded him again:

> "...'Look,' he said, 'I have a quarter of a shekel of silver. I will give it to the man of God so that he will tell us what way to take.'"
> - 1 Samuel 9:8

With humility, Saul agreed and that was the path that took him to Samuel, the man of God who anointed him as king (something much more than the lost donkeys). Therefore, a small opportunity may lead to a big opening. Do you know what lies ahead of you? Even if you do, you may not know how it would be done.

Lepers at the Entrance of the City Gate - 2 Kings 7

With severe famine in the land, these people had three options to choose from, each one leading to death, but only one had a little bit more to offer.

> "Now there were four men with leprosy at the entrance of the city gate. They said to each other, 'Why stay here until we die?
> 4 If we say, "We'll go into the city"- the famine is there, and we will die. And if we stay here, we will die. **So let's go over to the camp of the Arameans and surrender. If they spare us, we live; if they kill us, then we die.**'" - 2 Kings 7:3-4

In the end, they took the option where a small chance of survival existed.

> "The men who had leprosy reached the edge of the camp and entered one of the tents. They ate and drank, and carried away silver, gold and clothes, and went off and hid them. They returned and entered another tent and took some things from it and hid them also." - 2 Kings 7:8

The lepers were unselfish with their discovery, and they reported it to the royal palace. Guess what? They hid some goodies for themselves! Is that dealing wisely?

Jacob sought grain from Egypt.
Jacob made a decision similar to the lepers' (above) when there was famine in Egypt and Canaan.

> "When Jacob learned that there was grain in Egypt, he said to his sons, *'Why do you just keep looking at each other?'* ² He continued, 'I have heard that there is grain in Egypt. Go down there and buy some for us, so that we may live and not die.'" - Genesis 42:1-2

Jacob's children did as instructed and after a few trips to Egypt, they were all reunited with Joseph, who resettled them in Goshen. It was a small opportunity but it turned to a large opening. An opportunity may force you to relocate.

> "So Joseph settled his father and his brothers in Egypt and gave them property in the best part of the land, the district of Rameses, as Pharaoh directed." - Genesis 47:11

Sometimes an opportunity may arise and God may want you to relocate because there may not be room for you to flourish where you are. Take a look at Isaac's journey; he kept trying despite the angry disputes between his servants and the herdsmen of Gerar.

> *"Then they dug another well, but they quarrelled over that one also; so he named it Sitnah.*
> ²²*He moved on from there and dug another well, and no-one quarrelled over it. He named it Rehoboth, saying, 'Now the Lord has given us room and we will flourish in the land.'*
> ²³ *From there he went up to Beersheba."* - Genesis 26:21-23

Daniel put forward three for appointment.
Refer to Proverbs 22:29. If your God made you proud that a king fell at your feet, gave you a high position, and lavished you with many gifts, how would you use your position? After interpreting King Nebuchadnezzar's dream, Daniel saw an opportunity and unselfishly, he used it to elevate others.

> "⁴⁷ *The king said to Daniel, 'Surely your God is the God of gods and the Lord of kings and a revealer of mysteries, for you were able to reveal this mystery.'*
> ⁴⁸ *Then the king placed Daniel in a high position and lavished many gifts on him. He made him ruler over the entire province of Babylon and placed him in charge of all its wise men.*
> ⁴⁹*Moreover, at Daniel's request the king appointed Shadrach, Meshach and Abednego administrators over the province of Babylon, while Daniel himself remained at the royal court."*
>
>   - Daniel 2:47-49

Were Shadrach, Meshach, and Abednego qualified to be appointed as administrators? Yes (it is not nepotism). Look below:

> "The king talked with them, and he found none equal to Daniel, Hananiah, Mishael and Azariah; so they entered the king's service. [20] In every matter of wisdom and understanding about which the king questioned them, he found them **ten times better than all the magicians and enchanters in his whole kingdom.**" - Daniel 1:19-20

Again, the above shows: "The race is not to the swift or the battle to the strong, nor does food come to the wise or wealth to the brilliant or favour to the learned; but time and chance happen to them all." Listen to this:

> "As we have therefore opportunity, let us do good unto all men, especially unto them who are of the household of faith."
> - Galatians 6:10

A difficult thing is doable and stay close to those who can help you.

Let us examine Elisha's request for a double portion of Elijah's spiritual power. Twice Elisha was told, *"Do you know that the Lord is going to take your master from you today?"* (2 Kings 2:3, 5), and twice he answered, "Yes, I know." So Elisha refused to leave his master and an opportunity presented itself.

OPPORTUNITY: SENSE IT & GRAB IT | 175

> *"⁹When they had crossed, Elijah said to Elisha, 'Tell me, what can I do for you before I am taken from you?' 'Let me inherit a double portion of your spirit,' Elisha replied.*
> *¹⁰'You have asked a difficult thing,' Elijah said, 'yet if you see me when I am taken from you, it will be yours - otherwise not.'"*
>
> - 2 Kings 2:9-10

Sometimes a thing that is seen as difficult is doable. Therefore, do not hold back from trying or asking. Without being a pest, stay close to those who can help you.

How are the following connected to opportunity?
    Association ~ with God and people
    Ability ~ natural or acquired skill or talent
    Attitude ~ the way you behave
    Awareness ~ having knowledge of

With reference to the examples cited in this chapter and other relevant examples in the scriptures, discuss the above Quadruple A's (Association, Ability, Attitude, and Awareness) as they relate to opportunities.

Like Daniel and the lepers in two of the aforementioned examples, think of this:

> *"Each of you should look not only to your own interests, but also to the interests of others."* - Philippians 2:5

Obedience

If one can lay a good foundation, building upon such an underpinning will not be difficult. For a Christian, a good foundation is to be obedient. Look at the parable of the Wise and Foolish Builders in Luke 6:46-49; anyone who hears his (Christ's) words and puts them into practice is likened to a wise builder. According to Isaiah 33:6, Christ is the sure foundation of our times. This topic aims to address obedience as a behaviour intended to please God. That is, the condition or quality of being obedient to God's instructions. Obedience is not only observing the Ten Commandments; it is also doing what God, men of God, and our God-fearing parents say. We must also obey authorities.

A MATTER OF CHOICE!

With regard to God's commands and instructions, He gave us a choice:

> "If you are willing and obedient, you shall eat the good of the land." - Isaiah 1:19

In Deuteronomy 30:19-20, the issue of choice regarding obedience is made even clearer:

> *"I call heaven and earth to witness against you this day, that I have set before you life and death, blessing and curse; therefore choose*

life, that you and your descendants may live, loving the Lord your God, obeying his voice, and cleaving to him; for that means life to you and length of days, that you may dwell in the land which the Lord swore to your fathers, to Abraham, to Isaac, and to Jacob, to give them."

Before giving the Ten Commandments, God told Moses:

> "...If you listen carefully to the voice of the Lord your God and do what is right in his eyes, if you pay attention to his commands and keep all his decrees, I will not bring on you any of the diseases I brought on the Egyptians, for I am the Lord, who heals you."
>
> - Exodus 15:26-27

Again, the use of the word 'if' shows that God gave us a choice regarding his commandments.

Abraham obeyed the voice of God, kept his charge, commandments, statutes, and laws. If you believe that you were created by God, then make the right choice; obey Him.

WHO DO YOU OBEY?
Obey men of God.

There should be no doubt about obeying the instructions of God, but we are also to obey the instruction of God passed on by men of God. See 2 Chronicles 20:20 and Deuteronomy 18:21-22. We must also understand that men of God have the authority of God vested in them. But you must know that of a truth, he is a man of God. If a man of God tries to persuade you to follow other gods, do not listen or obey. To confirm this, read Deuteronomy 13:1-3.

Obey your parents/parents in the Lord.
The scriptures instruct that we listen to and heed the instructions of our parents. It says:

> "Children, obey your parents in the Lord, for this is right. 'Honour your father and mother' (this is the first commandment with a promise), 'that it may be well with you and that you may live long on the earth.'" - Ephesians 6:1-3.

Read Proverbs 4:1 and Proverbs 7:1-2. The example of the Recabites in Jeremiah 35 shows how successive generations obeyed parents' instructions. See also Colossians 3:20.

Obedience to parents has no age limitation and so does not exclude adults. Solomon obeyed his father's final instructions, but he applied wisdom in doing so. Read 1 Kings 2 especially verses 8-9 and 36-46. He placed Shimei under house arrest but later killed him for violating the detention. Solomon's reign may not have lasted long had he disregarded his father's instructions. The instruction to kill Joab (the defecting General) was also carried out by Solomon.

While in danger, Jacob obeyed his father's and mother's

instruction to flee. See Genesis 27:43-45, 28:7(below):

> "...and that Jacob had obeyed his father and mother and had gone to Paddan Aram."

On the other hand, Esau, his brother, deliberately disobeyed his parents. His wives made life unbearable for Isaac and Rebekah. Read Genesis 24:2-4, Genesis 26:34-35, Genesis 27:46, and Genesis 28:6-9.

From Obedience to the Palace: Saul was anointed king as he went looking for his father's lost donkeys. If he had refused to go searching for the missing animals, he would not have met Samuel, who anointed him as king (1 Samuel 9:3-27).

David got to know about Goliath when he took supplies to his brothers in the war front. Had he refused his father's instruction, he would have missed the opportunity to fight with and defeat Goliath, on whose life there was a great reward (1 Samuel 17:17-18, 25).

Obey authorities.
Imagine if everyone were left to do what he or she thinks is right! Life would be unbearable for the less privileged. It happened for a time in Israel: "In those days Israel had no king; everyone did as he saw fit" (Judges 21:25). Christians should be encouraged to embrace authorities so as to have freedom from quarrels and disagreement.

> "Let everyone be subject to the governing authorities, for there is no authority except that which God has established. The authorities that exist have been established by God. ²Consequently, whoever rebels against the authority is rebelling against what God has instituted, and those who do so will bring judgement on themselves." - Romans 13:1-2

Read also Titus 3:1 and Ephesians 6:5-8. With regard to obeying authorities, let the action of Shadrach, Meshach, and Abednego guide you. Daniel 3:12 reads:

> "There are certain Jews whom you have appointed over the affairs of the province of Babylon: Shadrach, Meshach, and Abednego. These men, O king, pay no heed to you; they do not serve your gods or worship the golden image which you have set up."

Also read Acts 5:25-29. You cannot obey man to disobey God.

Obey your husband.
If it were not necessary, the scriptures would not instruct women to do this:

> "Wives, be subject to your husbands, as to the Lord. For the husband is the head of the wife as Christ is the head of the church, his body, and is himself its Saviour" - Ephesians 5:22-23

But where do you draw the line? During a bible study session, a lady explained how she was persuaded by her husband not to pay her tithe since she was supporting a church project financially at that time. Although the Spirit of the Lord instructed her in a dream to pay her tithe, she did not and she lost her job.

The Blessings of Obedience

Assured blessing: See the verses under "A Matter of Choice" above. These two verses assure any believer of the blessing of obedience:

> "...the blessing if you obey the commands of the Lord your God that I am giving you today." - Deuteronomy 11:27

> "Now if you obey me fully and keep my covenant, then out of all nations you will be my treasured possession. Although the whole earth is mine..." - Exodus 19:5

Notice that the blessing or promise attached is conditional because of the use of the word 'if'. Read Leviticus 26:3-13 and Deuteronomy 28:1-14.

God will be an enemy to your enemy.

Look at Exodus 23:22:

> "If you listen carefully to what he says and do all that I say, I will be an enemy to your enemies and will oppose those who oppose you."

That is, God will fight for you. Many Christians still think they do not have enemies. Don't be naive. Christ as a newborn had an enemy in King Herod, while Joseph, a young seventeen-year-old boy, was sold into slavery by his own brothers.

Inherited blessings: God blessed Isaac because of Abraham. The same can apply to your children if you obey God. Look at Genesis 26:4-5:

> *"I will make your descendants as numerous as the stars in the sky and will give them all these lands, and through your offspring all nations on earth will be blessed,* 5 *because Abraham obeyed me and did everything I required of him, keeping my commands, my decrees, and my instructions."*

Upon the Recabites God pronounced a blessing for obeying the instructions passed down by their grandparents. Read Jeremiah 35:1-11, 18-19.

Draw strength from this:

> *"But the man who looks intently into the perfect law that gives freedom, and continues to do this, not forgetting what he has heard, but doing it - he will be blessed in what he does."* - James 1:25

PUNISHMENT FOR DISOBEDIENCE

There are several examples of disobedience in the bible and the consequences are too numerous to list. See Leviticus 26:14-35 for a few of them. The case of the prophet from Judah stands out. He was initially instructed by God on what to do in Bethel but disobeyed by being persuaded to do otherwise by an older prophet who was lying. The story is in 1 Kings 13.

When Saul disobeyed the instruction of Samuel (1 Samuel 13:8-14), he lost the kingdom. The Lord did not answer Saul when he inquired, neither by dreams nor through prophets. - 1 Samuel 27:6.

Lot's wife became a pillar of salt when she looked back, contrary to the instruction of the angel of the Lord. - Genesis 19:17, 26.

Obey not sacrifice.

After Saul disobeyed God's instruction with regard to punishing the Amalekites, Samuel said:

> *"Does the Lord delight in burnt offerings and sacrifices as much as in obeying the voice of the Lord. To obey is better than sacrifice, and to heed is better than the fat of rams."* - 1 Samuel 15:22

What God really wants from us is a contrite heart, not atonement with gifts to God for sins. Here, Saul made a mistake by pleasing men to disobey God. Was the survival of Israel dependent on the 'best sheep and oxen' Saul took as spoil? Remember also that:

"For as by one man's disobedience many were made sinners, so by the obedience of one shall many be made righteous."

- Romans 5:19

Because of the sin of Adam and Eve, the ground was cursed and women will bear children in pain, to say a few of the repercussions. See Genesis 3:16-19. For the obedience of Abraham, those who are of faith are blessed with the blessing of Abraham. Read Galatians 3:7-9. Indeed, through Abraham all the nations on earth are blessed with Jesus Christ.

"...and through your offspring all nations on earth will be blessed, because you have obeyed me." - Genesis 22:18

Wisdom

When you have the ability to make good judgement and give sound advice, you have wisdom. If you are bringing up children, running a business, leading a congregation, working, an adolescent person, or a servant, you need wisdom to succeed. Therefore, wisdom is essential for every human being because it is vital for good behaviour and useful in decision making. The scripture therefore says:

> "Get wisdom, get understanding; do not forget my words or turn away from them" - Proverbs 4:5

Wisdom is more than the knowledge acquired by intellectual means (formal education). It is a gift.

WHAT IS WISDOM?

This topic deals with Divine Wisdom not Earthly Wisdom. Take a look at James 3:13-16:

> "Who is wise and understanding among you? By his good life let him show his works in the meekness of wisdom. But if you have bitter jealousy and selfish ambition in your hearts, do not boast and be false to the truth. This wisdom is not such as comes down from above, but is earthly, unspiritual, devilish. For where jealousy and selfish ambition exist, there will be disorder and every vile

practice. But the wisdom from above is first pure, then peaceable, gentle, open to reason, full of mercy and good fruits, without uncertainty or insincerity."

If you look at Job 28:28:

"And he said to man, 'The fear of the Lord - that is wisdom, and to shun evil is understanding."

And Proverbs 9:10:

"The fear of the Lord is the beginning of wisdom, and knowledge of the Holy One is understanding."

Then one can conclude that possessing wisdom is having the fear of God.

Elihu made Job and his friends understand that wisdom:

"...is the spirit in a man, the breath of the Almighty, that gives him understanding." - Job 32:8

WHERE CAN WISDOM BE FOUND?

Draw a conclusion from these two bible references;
Job 28:12-21:

> "But where can wisdom be found? Where does understanding dwell? Man does not comprehend its worth; it cannot be found in the land of the living. ¹⁴ The deep says, 'It is not in me'; the sea says, 'It is not with me.' ... ²¹ It is hidden from the eyes of every living thing, concealed even from the birds of the air."

Ecclesiastes 7:24:

> "Whatever wisdom may be, it is far off and most profound - who can discover it?"

HOW TO GET WISDOM

Since wisdom is not something that is audible, visible, or tangible, you cannot see, feel, or touch it. So how can you obtain it? It is a spiritual gift that is divinely imparted unto man as God pleases. Isaiah 11:2 reads:

> "And the spirit of the Lord shall rest upon him, the spirit of wisdom and understanding, the spirit of counsel and might, the spirit of knowledge and of the fear of the Lord."

For insight, discuss these questions during bible study: ¹ Can a young person be wise and is wisdom obtained with age? ² Are great men always wise? It is important to note that anyone seeking to acquire wisdom must understand that it cannot be acquired overnight. Even with Jesus Christ, it increased as he grew up.

> "And Jesus grew in wisdom and stature, and in favour with God and man." - Luke 2:52

The following outlines how the wisdom of God can be obtained.

Have the fear of God.
It is probably the most important factor because the fear of God brings wisdom. Psalms 111:10 reads:

> "The fear of the Lord is the beginning of wisdom; all who follow his precepts have good understanding. To him belongs eternal praise."

Pray for wisdom.
If you need a loan, you will approach a bank or someone you know that has money. Applying the same principle, ask the One who can give you wisdom, God. Proverbs 2:6 reads:

> "For the Lord gives wisdom, and from his mouth come knowledge and understanding."

To substantiate this, see below how Christ gave understanding to his disciples.

> "Then he opened their minds so they could understand the Scriptures." - Luke 24:45

Solomon requested wisdom to judge (1 Kings 3:7-13) and God gave him wisdom that surpassed those of his time and those after him (verses 10-13). Look at Luke 11:13.

Heed good advice.
You will become wise or wiser as you listen to and consider good advice. Proverbs 13:10 says:

> *"Pride only breeds quarrels, but wisdom is found in those who take advice."*

David heeded good advice. In the issue between Nabal and David, David took about 400 men with swords to attack him (one unarmed man). Abigail rushed to stop him from attacking her husband, Nabal. She pleaded with David not to kill her husband. Look at Abigail's good advice to David in 1 Samuel 25:23-35. David also remembered her as she had requested (verses 31 and 39). Subsequent humiliation suffered by David was not avenged by David. (See 2 Samuel 10:4-5 and 2 Samuel 16:5-10.) He left it for God to do. David also refused to harm Saul despite the opportunity (1 Samuel 26:5-9).

Esther obtained favour from King Ahasuerus by requesting nothing, as advised by Hegai. Read Esther 2:15-17. Although godliness with contentment is great gain, Esther needed something special to beat other 'beautiful young virgins' to becoming the new queen. Beauty in a woman will fade away but the quality of contentment seen in Esther pleased King Ahasuerus. No wonder King Lemuel was told:

> "Charm is deceptive, and beauty is fleeting; but a woman who fears the Lord is to be praised." - Proverbs 31:30

Read the bible.
Observing God's commandments and understanding the Word will certainly make one wise or wiser. David said:

> "Your commands make me wiser than my enemies, for they are ever with me. ^{99}I have more insight than all my teachers, for I meditate on your statutes. ^{100}I have more understanding than the elders, for I obey your precepts. ^{101}I have kept my feet from every evil path so that I might obey your word." - Psalm 119:98-101

As Jesus Christ grew up, he went to the temple to listen to people teaching:

> "...they found him in the temple courts, sitting among the teachers, listening to them and asking them questions." - Luke 2:46

WISDOM IN RELATION TO SKILLS
God also gives wisdom in relation to skills. See Exodus 28:3:

> "Tell all the skilled men to whom I have given wisdom in such matters that they are to make garments for Aaron, for his consecration, so he may serve me as priest."

See 1 Kings 7:13-14. (Hiram was brought from Tyre by King Solomon for the bronze work in the temple.)

See Exodus 31:1-6. God gave wisdom, understanding, and knowledge in all manner of workmanship.

WISDOM IS A MAGNET

When you possess wisdom, it will draw people to you. This is evident in the two verses below.

> *"How happy your men must be! How happy your officials, who continually stand before you and hear your wisdom!"*
>
> *- 1 Kings 10:8*

> *"The whole world sought audience with Solomon to hear the wisdom God had put in his heart." - 1 Kings 10:24*

WISDOM CAN TAKE YOU TO A POSITION OF RESPONSIBILITY

Joseph's advice was good in the eyes of Pharaoh and to all his officials (Genesis 41:33-37). Thus, he was appointed as Pharaoh's deputy.

Ezra was instructed to appoint magistrates and judges:
> *"And you, Ezra, in accordance with the wisdom of your God, which you possess, appoint magistrates and judges to administer justice to all the people of Trans-Euphrates - all who know the laws of your God. And you are to teach any who do not know them."*
>
> *- Ezra 7:25*

Jethro advised Moses to choose men of truth and such that have the fear of God to be rulers of hundreds, fifties, and tens (Exodus 18:13-23). This implies that wisdom (through the fear of God) brought these men to positions of authority.

Ahithophel counseled King David and Absalom:

> "Now in those days the advice Ahithophel gave was like that of one who inquires of God. That was how both David and Absalom regarded all of Ahithophel's advice." - 2 Samuel 16:23

This statement caps it all:

> "Do you see a man skilled in his work? He will serve before kings; he will not serve before obscure men." - Proverbs 22:29

WISDOM IN DECISION MAKING

Below are a few examples of wise decisions:
- Solomon's wise judgement in 1 Kings 3:23-28
- Joseph showed restraint by not sleeping with Potiphar's wife in Genesis 39:7-10. This was before the Ten Commandments.
- Christ's judgement regarding the woman caught in adultery in John 8:3-10. In this example, the scribes and Pharisees tested Christ so that they might accuse him of something. But they were convicted by their conscience by the question raised in verse John 8:7.

WISDOM WILL SAVE YOU

Looking at these two examples, applying wisdom will preserve your life. While running away from trouble, David pretended to be insane before Achish king of Gath, despite the accolade he received for his bravery (1 Samuel 21:10-15). Abraham 'deceived' Abimelech concerning Sarah, his wife. He said, "She is my sister." Was Abraham lying or just dealing wisely so he could live? Read Genesis 20.

Let us look at 1 Samuel 16:1-5. Was Samuel afraid or dealing wisely? Or did God make an excuse for Samuel? Are you intrigued?

Proverbs 2:12 - Wisdom will save you from the ways of wicked men, from men whose words are perverse.

Proverbs 4:6 - Do not forsake wisdom, and she will protect you; love her, and she will watch over you.

Proverbs 19:8 - He who gets wisdom loves his own soul; he who cherishes understanding prospers.

Ecclesiastes 7:12 - Wisdom is a shelter as money is a shelter, but the advantage of knowledge is this: that wisdom preserves the life of its possessor.

WISDOM'S 'HOUSEMATES'!

When you possess wisdom, other gifts come with it.

> "I, wisdom, dwell together with **prudence**; I possess **knowledge and discretion**." - Proverbs 8:12

> "When pride comes, then comes disgrace, but with **humility** comes wisdom." - Proverbs 11:2

DON'T BOAST

If you have acquired wisdom, do not boast. Jeremiah 9:23 reads:

> "Let not the wise boast of their wisdom or the strong boast of their strength or the rich boast of their riches."

A FOOLISH DECISION!

Look at Saul's foolish oath in 1 Samuel 14:24. Imagine this! A fighting army was made to fast and they became faint. Obviously, without food they would be tired and hungry. They later ate meat with blood (1 Samuel 14:31-33), which is an abomination to the Lord.

Faith

"...faith is being sure of what we hope for and certain of what we do not see." - Hebrews 11:1

How would you convince someone to worship a God that he or she cannot see or assure someone in hardship that there will soon be relief? It is only by faith.

A MEASURE OF FAITH REQUIRED

Although faith cannot be seen, the measure of faith we are required to have is about the size of a mustard seed. Small indeed but it can move a 'mountain'.

Regarding the demon-possessed boy brought before Christ. The disciples asked,

> "Why couldn't we drive it out? He replied, 'Because you have so little faith. Truly I tell you, if you have faith as small as a mustard seed, you can say to this mountain, Move from here to there, and it will move. Nothing will be impossible for you.'" - Matthew 17:19-20

A measure of faith is evident in this statement:

> "For by the grace given me I say to every one of you: Do not think of yourself more highly than you ought, but rather think of yourself with sober judgement, in accordance with the measure of faith God has given you." - Romans 12:3

HOW TO DEVELOP FAITH

Pray for it.

Faith is a spiritual gift. Therefore, a person seeking to have it must long to possess it. We can reason this out from 1 Corinthians 12:9: "to another faith by the same Spirit, to another gifts of healing by that one Spirit." Then 1 Corinthians 12:31 reads, "Now eagerly desire the greater gifts..." Therefore, pray for it.

1 Thessalonians 3:10 reads,
> "Night and day we pray most earnestly that we may see you again and supply what is lacking in your faith."

Seek the word.

To acquire faith, you need to listen to and receive the word of God with meekness. Ascertain this from this bible quotation:

> "Consequently, faith comes from hearing the message, and the message is heard through the word about Christ." - Romans 10:17

See also Acts 4:4:
> "But many who heard the message believed; so the number of men who believed grew to about five thousand."

1 Thessalonians 1:8 reads,
> "The Lord's message rang out from you not only in Macedonia and Achaia - your faith in God has become known everywhere. Therefore we do not need to say anything about it."

Meditate on examples in the scriptures that may be relevant to your situation. Remember, David approached Goliath only in the name of God; the smaller man, David, prevailed (1 Samuel 17:45). When there was no weapon, Jonathan and his armour bearer prevailed against an army (1 Samuel 14:6-7, 8-20).

Always put in mind that "The name of the Lord is a fortified tower; the righteous run to it and are safe" (Proverbs 18:10). See also Psalm 119:99 and Psalm 61:1-3.

HOW IMPORTANT IS FAITH?
You need faith to please God. Hebrews 11:6 reads:

> "...without faith it is impossible to please God, because anyone who comes to him must believe that he exists and that he rewards those who earnestly seek him."

CATEGORIES OF FAITH
Little Faith
Examples of what Christ identified as Little Faith:
Christ's disciples were afraid of the storm.
Matthew 8:26 - "'You of little faith, why are you so afraid?' Then he got up and rebuked the winds and the waves, and it was completely calm."

Why you should not worry:
Matthew 6:28-30 - "If that is how God clothes the grass of the field, which is here today and tomorrow is thrown into the fire, will he not much more clothe you - you of little faith?"

Jesus walked on the water but Peter could not.
Matthew 14:31 - "Immediately Jesus reached out his hand and caught him. 'You of little faith,' he said, why did you doubt?'"

When the disciples forgot to take bread along:
Matthew 16:8 - "Aware of their discussion, Jesus asked, 'You of little faith, why are you talking among yourselves about having no bread?'"

Great Faith

Examples of what Christ considered Great Faith:
The Centurion whose servant lay at home paralyzed simply requested Jesus say a word.
Matthew 8:7-10 - "When Jesus heard this, He was amazed and said to those following him, 'Truly I tell you, I have not found anyone in Israel with such great faith.'"

A Canaanite woman whose daughter was demon-possessed and suffering terribly:
Matthew 15:28 - "Then Jesus said to her, 'Woman, you have great faith! Your request is granted.' And her daughter was healed at that moment."

WHEN YOU HAVE FAITH ADD...

Having only faith is not enough; the scriptures recommend adding charity (love). Take a look at the following references.

> "And now these three remain: faith, hope and love. But the greatest of these is love." - 1 Corinthians 13:13

"But since you excel in everything - in faith, in speech, in knowledge, in complete earnestness, and in the love we have kindled in you - see that you also excel in this grace of giving." - 2 Corinthians 8:7

"The goal of this command is love, which comes from a pure heart and a good conscience and a sincere faith." - 1 Timothy 1:5

Look at 2 Peter 1:5-8 also.

FACTORS THAT CAN WORK AGAINST FAITH

Fear: Peter started well when he was walking on water, but once he exercised fear, he began to sink (Matthew 14:25-3).

Doubt: See Matthew 21:21:

"Jesus replied, 'Truly I tell you, if you have faith and do not doubt, not only can you do what was done to the fig tree, but also you can say to this mountain, Go, throw yourself into the sea, and it will be done.'"

High Expectation: Look at the example of Naaman in 2 Kings 5:5-14 (essentially verses 11-12). Elisha's prescription was below expectation. Naaman suggested two things Elisha should have said. The question I would like to ask Naaman is: Why consult a genuine man of God when you are not ready to do whatever he tells you to do?

Remember this! When wine ran out at the wedding to which Jesus and his disciples had been invited, Mary the mother of Jesus said to the servants, "Do whatever he tells you." (John 2:5). It is important that you do not lean on your own understanding.

Delay by Evil Forces: Proverbs 13:12 says, "Hope deferred makes the heart sick..." Also read Daniel 10:12-13.

PEOPLE WITH FAITH
- Shadrach, Meshach, and Abednego - Daniel 3
- The Syrophoenician woman - Mark 7:26
- The Centurion - Matthew 8:8-10
- Blind Bartimaeus - Mark 10:51
- And Stephen, full of faith and power, did great wonders and miracles among the people. - Acts 6:8

See also Hebrews 11 for examples of men and women who had faith.

WHAT FAITH CAN DO FOR A CHURCH

Good news spreads fast. A congregation will increase as the faith of the worshippers increases. There will be more answered prayers and testimonies. God's mercies and works cannot be hidden. Look at the following references:

> "He was a good man, full of the Holy Spirit and faith, and a great number of people were brought to the Lord." - Acts 11:24

> "So the churches were strengthened in the faith and grew daily in numbers." - Acts 16:5

FAITH BREEDS CONFIDENCE

Let us examine the case of David versus Goliath. What drove the young man to believe he could defeat Goliath, a war veteran? Goliath's weaponry includes a bronze javelin and spear with a shaft like a weaver's rod. And David's weaponry? A mere sling and a stone probably good enough to stun a medium-sized bird.

Before Goliath, David had killed a lion and bear. What he did next was put Goliath in the same category as these animals.

> "Your servant has killed both the lion and the bear; this uncircumcised Philistine will be like one of them, because he has defied the armies of the living God." - 1 Samuel 17:36

Was David trying to operate within the Genesis 1:28 command so that he could have dominion over Goliath? To top it all, he approached him using the name of God.

> "...but I come against you in the name of the Lord Almighty, the God of the armies of Israel, whom you have defied."
>
> - 1 Samuel 17:45

Here, David's understanding of the God of Israel was put to use. That is, the Lord is a warrior (Exodus 15:3). David also ran quickly to the battle line. That is, you cannot be sluggish with your faith. To develop faith, your understanding of the might of God is essential. 1 John 5:14 says,

> "This is the confidence we have in approaching God: that if we ask anything according to his will, he hears us."

LACK OF FAITH HINDERS WORK

Imagine an aircraft hovering without anywhere to land. Power moves through faith whether it be power of accomplishment, victory, healing, or success. When faith is lacking, little is achieved.

Matthew 13:58 reads, "And he did not do many miracles there because of their lack of faith."

1 Timothy 1:19 reads, "...holding on to faith and a good conscience, which some have rejected and so have suffered shipwreck with regard to the faith."

YOU ARE JUSTIFIED BY FAITH

Galatians 2:15-16 says:
> "We who are Jews by birth and not sinful Gentiles know that a person is not justified by observing the law, but by faith in Jesus Christ. So we, too, have put our faith in Christ Jesus that we may be justified by faith in Christ and not by observing the law, because by observing the law no one will be justified."

Ephesians 2:8 reads,

> *"For it is by grace you have been saved, through faith - and this is not from yourselves, it is the gift of God."*

FAITH FOUND IN THREE GENERATIONS

Three generations of Timothy were found to have faith in God.

> *"I am reminded of your sincere faith, which first lived in your grandmother Lois and in your mother Eunice and, I am persuaded, now lives in you also."* - 2 Timothy 1:5

Now, pass on your faith.

Humility

Humility is the quality or condition of being humble. Humble people are usually marked by their meekness and modesty in attitude or behaviour; they are not proud or arrogant. To receive the grace of God in abundance, one needs to show humility to God because...

> *"...God opposes the proud but shows favour to the humble."*
>
> - 1 Peter 5:5

HUMILITY AS A REQUIREMENT

> *"He has shown you, O mortal, what is good. And what does the Lord require of you? To act justly and to love mercy and to walk humbly with your God." - Micah 6:8*

With a lowly heart, God will show you the right path. Psalms 25:9 reads:

> *"He leads the humble in what is right, and teaches the humble his way."*

Paul, in his account to the elders in Ephesus, said,

> *"When they arrived, he said to them: 'You know how I lived the whole time I was with you, from the first day I came into the province of Asia. [19] I served the Lord with great humility and with*

tears and in the midst of severe testing by the plots of my Jewish opponents..." - Acts 20:18-19

HUMILITY WILL TURN AWAY THE WRATH OF GOD

Humility often turns away the wrath of God. Hezekiah was ungrateful after recovering from an illness but humbled himself to turn away the wrath of God.

> *"But Hezekiah's heart was proud and he did not respond to the kindness shown him; therefore the Lord's wrath was on him and on Judah and Jerusalem. [26] Then Hezekiah repented of the pride of his heart, as did the people of Jerusalem; therefore the Lord's wrath did not come on them during the days of Hezekiah."*
>
> - 2 Chronicles 32:25-26

ASSOCIATE WITH HUMBLE PEOPLE

Since *...with humility comes wisdom* (Proverbs 11:2), the scripture recommends that we associate with humble people.

> *"Live in harmony with one another. Do not be proud, but be willing to associate with people of low position. Do not be conceited[b]."*
>
> - Romans 12:16

b) **Conceited** means having an excessively high opinion of oneself.

CHRIST AS AN EXAMPLE

The examples shown by Christ are remarkable. He has power

and might. The whole earth and everything in it belongs to Him, yet he was associated with the following:

At birth he was laid in a manger:

> "...and she gave birth to her firstborn, a son. She wrapped him in cloths and placed him in a manger, because there was no guest room available for them." - Luke 2:7

Imagine, there was no room for a man whose Father's house has many mansions (John 14:2). The whole earth is also his and he could have chosen to be born in the Buckingham Palace or London's Harley Street equivalent of those days.

His native town was a small place:

To make a statement, Jesus Christ could have been born in the biggest city on earth. Instead he was born in small town called Bethlehem.

> "But you, Bethlehem Ephrathah, though you are small among the clans of Judah, out of you will come for me one who will be ruler over Israel, whose origins are from of old, from ancient times."
> - Micah 5:2

He rode on an ass instead of a chariot plated with gold:

> "'Say to Daughter Zion, 'See, your king comes to you, gentle and riding on a donkey, and on a colt, the foal of a donkey.' ⁶ The

disciples went and did as Jesus had instructed them. ⁷They brought the donkey and the colt and placed their cloaks on them for Jesus to sit on." - Matthew 21:5-7

In the form of God but decided to come as a man:
See Philippians 2:3-10.

He ate with sinners and tax collectors; no discrimination:
While Jesus was having dinner at Matthew's house, many tax collectors and sinners came and ate with him and his disciples. ¹¹When the Pharisees saw this, they asked his disciples, 'Why does your teacher eat with tax collectors and sinners?'"
— Matthew 9:10-11

HUMILITY IN SERVICE /THE BODY OF CHRIST
Aaron was Moses' older brother, but he served under Moses. Aaron was also alive when Joshua was inaugurated to lead Israel. They never disrespected Aaron. Young people in the service of the Lord must show humility.

To the elders:
"Be shepherds of God's flock that is under your care, watching over them - not because you must, but because you are willing, as God wants you to be; not pursuing dishonest gain, but eager to serve; not lording it over those entrusted to you, but being examples to the flock." - 1 Peter 5:2-3.

To the young ones:
> "...you who are younger, submit yourselves to your elders. All of you, clothe yourselves with humility toward one another, because 'God opposes the proud but shows favour to the humble.' ⁶Humble yourselves, therefore, under God's mighty hand, that he may lift you up in due time." - 1 Peter 5:5-6

HUMILITY IN RELATIONSHIPS

To discuss this, have in mind that to be humble is to show deferential or submissive respect. 1 Peter 2:17 says:

> "Show proper respect to everyone..."

Between husband and wife

Simple: For the husband is the head of the wife as Christ is the head of the church, his body, and is himself its Savior - Ephesians 5:23-(33). However, let each one of you love his wife as himself, and let the wife see that she respects her husband. Read 1 Timothy 3:4 and Colossians 3:18-19 as well.

Between parents and children

Children must respect their parents while parents and guardians must guard against abuse. Read Leviticus 19:3, Ephesians 6:1-4, and Colossians 3:20-21. Leviticus 19:32 says:

> "Stand up in the presence of the aged, show respect for the elderly, and revere your God. I am the Lord."

Between siblings

For any family to live in harmony, there must be respect amongst siblings. The elder should not take advantage of the younger, and the younger must respect the elder. Parents and guardians have a duty to see that this is done. Charity begins at home, they say.

Between employer and employee

Even if you are older than your boss or employer and/or more qualified than him or her, as a Christian, you must show humility. Bosses and employers must not abuse authority and they should have in mind that there is promotion for the lowly. 1 Samuel 2:7 says, "The Lord sends poverty and wealth; he humbles and he exalts." Read Ephesians 6:5-9 and Colossians 3:21-23. Also:

> *"Do nothing out of selfish ambition or vain conceit, but in humility consider others better than yourselves." - Philippians 2:3*

Consider adding honesty to your humility. Do you have integrity like that of Jacob? To Laban, Jacob said:

> *"And my honesty will testify for me in the future..." - Genesis 30:33*

WHAT PRIDE DOES

Pride is one of the seven things the Lord detests (Proverbs 6:16). It also leads to a fall as:

> *"Pride goes before destruction, a haughty spirit before a fall."*
> *- Proverbs 16:18*

This is evident in the case of King Nebuchadnezzar. See Daniel 4:28-37. His son was also not humble. - Daniel 5:20, 22-23

Queen Vashti was dethroned because of her pride (Esther 1:10-22). Indeed, pride goes before a fall.

Remember, a man's pride will bring him low, but he who is lowly in spirit will obtain honour. - Proverbs 29:23. See the parable of the Pharisee and the Publican in Luke 18:11-14.

WARNING!
If you are rich, don't be proud (1 Timothy 6:17-19).
If you are successful, don't be proud (Deuteronomy 8:11-17).

Also read Proverbs 30:7-9.

Dealing with Anger

Anger is cruel and fury overwhelming, but who can stand before jealousy?
- Proverbs 27:4

Anger is simply defined as a feeling of extreme annoyance or displeasure. Displeasure may be brought about through things such as remarks, hatred, and jealousy. The cognitive behaviour theory attributes anger to several factors such as past experiences, behaviour learned from others, genetic predispositions, and a lack of problem-solving ability.

According to the Rational Emotive Behaviour Therapy (REBT), introduced in 1955 by Albert Ellis, irrational evaluative beliefs such as "Things must be the way I want," or "Others must do what I tell them to do," combined with a low-frustration tolerance (LFT) (e.g., "if they don't do it I can't stand it"), cause anger and lead to aggressive behaviour.

Making foolish remarks such as 'bitch,' 'f*** you,' 'bastard,' or similar expletives can trigger anger in vulnerable people. But the scripture advised thus: "But just as he who called you is holy, so be holy in all you do." - 1 Peter 1:15

And Proverbs 26:4 says: "Do not answer a fool according to his folly, or you yourself will be just like him."

AVOID MAKING PEOPLE ANGRY

As Christians, the first step to take in dealing with anger is to avoid making people angry. Carefully choose your words. In some cases, keeping quiet may be even better so as to avoid strife. Remarks like 'Who are you?' or 'Who do you think you are?' should be avoided.

Nabal enraged King David by this remark:

> "Who is this David? Who is this son of Jesse? Many servants are breaking away from their masters these days." - 1 Samuel 25:10

The above is not the kind of reply one would expect from a person to whom you sent this type of greeting:

> "Long life to you! Good health to you and your household! And good health to all that is yours!" - 1 Samuel 25:5-6

But the scriptures say in Proverbs 15:1, "A gentle answer turns away wrath, but a harsh word stirs up anger."

Also James 1:19 reads, "My dear brothers, take note of this: Everyone should be quick to listen, slow to speak, and slow to become angry..."

SHOW RESTRAINT WHEN ANGRY

Another way of dealing with anger is to show restraint (control or repression of feelings). Be wise and look at the following references:

Psalm 37:8 - Refrain from anger and turn from wrath; do not fret - it leads only to evil.

Ecclesiastes 7:9 - Do not be quickly provoked in your spirit, for anger resides in the lap of fools.

Proverbs 29:8 - Mockers stir up a city, but wise men turn away anger.

Proverbs 29:11 - Fools give full vent to their rage, but the wise bring calm in the end.

WHO IS YOUR FRIEND?

People pick up habits from others. If the cognitive behaviour theory attributes anger to factors such as behaviour learned from others, then do not keep the company of anyone who is easily angered.

> "Do not make friends with a hot-tempered person, do not associate with one easily angered, or you may learn their ways and get yourself ensnared." - Proverbs 22:24-25

If you are not convinced, look at this:

> "Do not be misled: 'Bad company corrupts good character.'"
> - 1 Corinthians 15:33

IN YOUR ANGER, DO NOT SIN

Ephesians 4:26 says, "In your anger do not sin: Do not let the sun go down while you are still angry."

Amongst other things, Saul's anger toward David caused him to sin. Listen to this:

> "Saul was very angry; this refrain displeased him greatly. 'They have credited David with tens of thousands,' he thought, 'but me with only thousands. What more can he get but the kingdom?'"
> - 1 Samuel 18:8

GET RID OF IT

Anger is one spirit you cannot afford to keep. It does not add value to anyone who has it. Look at the following verses:

> "But now you must rid yourselves of all such things as these: anger, rage, malice, slander, and filthy language from your lips."
> - Colossians 3:8

> "Get rid of all bitterness, rage and anger, brawling and slander, along with every form of malice." - Ephesians 4:31

Also listen to correction or pleas. See Abigail's good advice to David in 1 Samuel 25:23-35. Quite a number of people in prisons today would look back and regret not taking correction or listening to pleas.

FORGIVENESS IS KEY

The scripture says,

> "Whoever would foster love covers over an offense, but whoever repeats the matter separates close friends." - Proverbs 17:9

Do not keep referring to past offenses. Could this be where the popular phrase 'Forgive and forget' was coined?

ANGER IN RELATIONSHIPS

Anger is one of the most common negative features in relationships. If not carefully managed, it can degenerate into loss of affection, violence, etc. Guard against picking up quarrel on issues beyond your partner's control.

Listen to this:

> "When Rachel saw that she bore Jacob no children, she envied her sister; and she said to Jacob, **'Give me children, or I shall die!'** Jacob's anger was kindled against Rachel, and he said, 'Am I in the place of God, who has withheld from you the fruit of the womb?'"
>
> - Genesis 30:1-2

Here, Jacob spoke with wisdom because Rachel was made barren:

> "When the Lord saw that Leah was not loved, he enabled her to conceive, but Rachel remained childless." - Genesis 29:31

If you were Jacob, how would you have answered?

SEVEN REASONS WHY YOU MUST CONTROL ANGER

1. For man's anger does not bring about the righteous life that God desires (James 1:20). See also Matthew 5:22.
2. Anger may cause you to lose friends.
3. It may make you lose your job, position, or throne.
4. Anger may be injurious to your health. The physical effects of anger include increased heart rate, blood pressure, and levels of adrenaline and noradrenalin. "Arrhythmia, also known as irregular heartbeat, can be triggered by anger and other strong emotions in vulnerable people."
5. It may destabilize a relationship.
6. Anger may demean you.
7. It may cause you to destroy property, harm, or kill. Eventually, it may lead to a prison or death sentence.

Think of these two verses always:

> "If it is possible, as far as it depends on you, live at peace with everyone." - Romans 12:18

And:

> "Make every effort to live in peace with everyone and to be holy; without holiness no one will see the Lord." - Hebrews 12:14

Forgiveness

It is befitting to discuss this topic just after treating "Dealing with Anger."

Why do we need to forgive?

Apart from being a good choice to make, it is also because:

> "...if you forgive other people when they sin against you, your heavenly Father will also forgive you. ¹⁵But if you do not forgive others their sins, your Father will not forgive your sins."
>
> - Matthew 6:14-15

Discuss the following:

Why must we forgive?

Think of a period when you were holding a grudge against someone who has caused you injury or insulted you. How did you feel then? You may have thought of retaliating (return like for like), or you may have chosen not to talk to the person again (i.e., to keep malice).

Then think of the time you have let go of your anger. You must have felt light-hearted. We must understand that "...disputes are like the barred gates of a citadel" (Proverbs 18:19). Communicating with someone you have a grudge with is restricted until you let go.

How do you forgive?

Refrain from telling everyone close to you about it. However, seek advice from a person who will advise you correctly; not a person who will fuel the feud. Again, read Proverbs 17:9.

If you are offended by a member of the church, take your matter to the elders:

> *"Therefore, if you have disputes about such matters, appoint as judges even men of little account in the church!"*
>
> - 1 Corinthians 6:4

Should you ask for forgiveness?

If you have offended a person, it will be right to ask for forgiveness when it is appropriate to do so. Let us look at some examples.

Jacob sent Joseph's brothers to seek forgiveness. See Genesis 50:17:

> *"This is what you are to say to Joseph: 'I ask you to forgive your brothers the sins and the wrongs they committed in treating you so badly.' Now please forgive the sins of the servants of the God of your father."*

When their message came to him, Joseph wept.

Saul also wept when David spared his life (1 Samuel 24: 16-19). Read Romans 12:14-18 as well.

Try this!

A gift given in secret soothes anger (Proverbs 21:14). I tried this when I was deemed to have offended a man of God. I was instructed in a dream to present him with a gift. It worked for me, and it afforded me the opportunity to explain to him the reason for my action for which he took offense. The relationship between me and that man of God improved from then onward. If you see anyone who cannot apologize or seek forgiveness, such a person is proud.

How many times should you forgive?

Many of us do set a limit for friends, relations, or colleagues. We even tell them once they have used up 'their credit,' so to say. Like Peter, the question often come to mind especially when one is dealing with 'persistent offenders'. Peter questioned Christ in Matthew 18:21-22:

> "...'Lord, how many times shall I forgive my brother when he sins against me? Up to seven times?' Jesus answered, 'I tell you, not seven times, but seventy-seven times.'"

Forgiveness encourages unity. Look at Colossians 3:12-14:

> "Therefore, as God's chosen people, holy and dearly loved, clothe yourselves with compassion, kindness, humility, gentleness, and patience. ¹³Bear with each other and forgive whatever grievances you may have against one another. Forgive as the Lord forgave you. ¹⁴And over all these virtues put on love, which binds them all together in perfect unity."

Making Vows

When we make an earnest promise to perform a specified act or behave in a certain manner in the church or before God, it is a vow. This is a good topic to start the year in a bible class. Don't we all make promises at the beginning of the year? It is not only when we do not keep the Ten Commandments that we sin. Some Christians often make mistakes by deferring, delaying, or not fulfilling their vows. This is counted as sin by God. Let us look at Ecclesiastes 5:4-6:

> "When you make a vow to God, do not delay to fulfill it. He has no pleasure in fools; fulfill your vow. It is better not to make a vow than to make one and not fulfill it. Do not let your mouth lead you into sin. And do not protest to the temple messenger, 'My vow was a mistake.' Why should God be angry at what you say and destroy the work of your hands?"

Faced with the possibility of defeat in the hands of the Ammonites, Jephthah, the mighty man of valour, made a vow to the Lord saying:

> "...If you give the Ammonites into my hands, whatever comes out of the door of my house to meet me when I return in triumph from the Ammonites will be the Lord's, and I will sacrifice it as a burnt offering." - Judges 11:30-31

The Lord gave him victory over the Ammonites, but when Jephthah returned to his home in Mizpah, his daughter was the first living thing to meet him.

> *"When Jephthah returned to his home in Mizpah, who should come out to meet him but his daughter, dancing to the sound of tambourines! She was an only child."* - Judges 11:34-37

Jephthah was disappointed, but his daughter encouraged him to pay his vow.

> *"...Do to me just as you promised, now that the Lord has avenged you of your enemies..."*

In another example, Hannah who was childless because the Lord closed her womb, in bitterness of soul wept and prayed to the Lord for a child. She also made a vow saying:

> *"...Lord Almighty, if you will only look on your servant's misery and remember me, and not forget your servant but give her a son, then I will give him to the Lord for all the days of his life, and no razor will ever be used on his head."* - 1 Samuel 1:10-11

Hannah did fulfill her vow by dedicating the boy, Samuel, to the Lord's service. Read 1 Samuel 1:24-28. Now, what did God give to Hannah for giving Samuel to the Lord's service as promised?

> "...And the Lord was gracious to Hannah; she conceived and gave birth to three sons and two daughters. Meanwhile, the boy Samuel grew up in the presence of the Lord." - 1 Samuel 2:19-21

Jacob also made a vow while fleeing from Esau his brother, saying:

> "...If God will be with me and will watch over me on this journey I am taking and will give me food to eat and clothes to wear so that I return safely to my father's house, then the Lord will be my God and this stone that I have set up as a pillar will be God's house, and of all that you give me I will give you a tenth."
>
> - Genesis 28:20-22

It is amazing that Jacob's vow was fulfilled by obeying God's instruction. Was God helping Jacob? He made the vow when he was a young man, but he fulfilled it while returning home with his family. At the time Jacob fulfilled his vow, Dinah, his tenth child, was old enough to get married. Read Genesis 35:1-7. Notice that God blessed Jacob after fulfilling his vow. Read Genesis 35:9-13.

In the three examples above, one can deduce that vows are made:
- In the time of hardship
- When you desire success
- In a situation in which something is required or wanted

Also notice that no timescale was attached to the requests. It will be wise not to attach a timescale when making a request. Can anyone instruct the Almighty God?

But making pledges to seek the praise of men, especially in the church, can be dangerous. The story of Ananias and his wife, Sapphira (Acts 5:1-10), tells it all. To understand what they were trying to do, read Acts 4:32-37. The best thing is to pledge only what you can give.

The scriptures encourage us to pay our vows.
The instructions in the bible verses listed below show that we are encouraged to pay our vows.
Numbers 30:2 -
> "When a man makes a vow to the Lord or takes an oath to obligate himself by a pledge, he must not break his word but must do everything he said."

Deuteronomy 23:21-23 -
> "If you make a vow to the Lord your God, do not be slow to pay it, for the Lord your God will certainly demand it of you and you will be guilty of sin. But if you refrain from making a vow, you will not be guilty..."

Psalms 116:14 -
> "I will fulfill my vows to the Lord in the presence of all His people."

Matthew 5:33 -

> "Again, you have heard that it was said to the people long ago, 'Do not break your oath, but fulfill to the Lord the vows you have made.'"

You must not pay your vow with something that has a defect.

> "If any of you - whether an Israelite or a foreigner residing in Israel - presents a gift for a burnt offering to the Lord, either to fulfill a vow or as a freewill offering... Do not bring anything with a defect, because it will not be accepted on your behalf."
>
> - Leviticus 22:18-21

Do not reflect after making or fulfilling your vow.

> "It is a trap to dedicate something rashly and only later to consider one's vows." - Proverbs 20:25

It is only when you have the fear of God that you can make a vow and pay it.

Moral Maxims 1

Proverbs 25

No country's constitution will teach you moral excellence, but you will find in it the principles on which a nation is governed. The bible, however, contains commandments, ordinances, and laws that will help us live peaceably with our neighbours. In the bible you will also find recommendations, observations, and ways to behave that constitute moral excellence. Various virtues can be found in the books of Proverbs and Ecclesiastes. I have chosen Proverbs 25-29 for the Moral Maxims series. To explain this chapter, verses similar in meaning are batched together under a short description.

God's intentions are unsearchable:

Verses 2-3: The secret things belong to God. The things we do not know are to the glory of God. So also, the hearts of kings are unsearchable. Look at Amos 3:7:

> "Surely the Sovereign Lord does nothing without revealing his plan to his servants the prophets."

That is, God tells us what he wants to do but he seldom tells us how he will do it. Take a look at Joseph's dreams in Genesis 37:5-9. God's intention concerning Joseph was made known in the dreams, but the way it would happen was not revealed. God did not reveal to Joseph that he would be sold to slavery and imprisoned for two years for an offense he did not commit. God may have given you a promise through a dream or prophecy; the way it will be accomplished may not have been revealed. This makes the ways of the Lord truly mysterious.

While in Egypt, the Israelites were promised a land flowing with milk and honey, but there was no mention of the wars and other problems they faced. Exodus 3:8 says:

> "So I have come down to rescue them from the hand of the Egyptians and to bring them up out of that land into a good and spacious land, a land flowing with milk and honey - the home of the Canaanites, Hittites, Amorites, Perizzites, Hivites, and Jebusites."

Can you imagine this complaint from a people God was to bless? Exodus 14:11 reads:

> "They said to Moses, 'Was it because there were no graves in Egypt that you brought us to the desert to die? What have you done to us by bringing us out of Egypt?'"

A wise king will have several advisers, but only the king himself will know in his own heart the decision he will make. Proverbs 11:14 reads: Where no counsel is, the people fall: but in the multitude of counselors there is safety.

Prepare yourself for the Master's use - Verse 4: Dross (the scum that forms on the surface of molten metal as a result of oxidation), once removed, brings out the shining qualities of a metal. Following the same principle, if you do away with your bad deeds, you will be an instrument for noble purposes (2 Timothy 2:19-21).

Moral uprightness is vital for rulers - Verse 5: When you remove wicked people who are around a king, his throne will be established. For example, Joab and Adonijah were executed to establish King Solomon's throne. Complementing this is Proverbs 16:12.

Don't boast before a king or a highly placed person and do not go and seat yourself in high places first. Wait to be called to take a seat (verses 6-7). See Luke 14:8-11. Read 2 Samuel 1:6-16 regarding the young man who boasted to David that he killed Saul. How did Saul die, and was the young man thinking that David would be excited to hear about the death of his enemy, Saul?

A gossip usually betrays - Verse 8-10.
Proverbs 11:13 - A gossip betrays a confidence, but a trustworthy man keeps a secret.

Carefully choose your words -Verse 11: A man finds joy in giving an apt reply, and how good is a timely word! - Proverbs 15:23

Comparisons / Observations:

Verses 12-14, 18-20, and 26 - Verse 18 says that like a club or a sword or a sharp arrow is the man who gives false testimony against his neighbour. The Lord hates it (Proverbs 6:16).
Proverbs 19:5 says, "A false witness will not go unpunished, and he who pours out lies will not go free." Also see Proverbs 14:5.

Verse 19 points out that like a bad tooth or a lame foot is reliance on the unfaithful in times of trouble. Simply put your trust in God. A man can disappoint you.

Soft words and patience are recommended to get results. As Verse 15 says, through patience a ruler can be persuaded, and a gentle tongue can break a bone. Is the scripture talking about 'peaceful protest'? See also Proverbs 15:1.

Exercise self-control as suggested in Verse 16: If you find honey, eat just enough - too much of it, and you will vomit.
Likewise, Verse 28 warns that like a city whose walls are broken down is a man who lacks self-control.

Anyone who lacks the ability to exercise restraint or control over his/her feelings, emotions, reactions, etc. will have the tendency to make mistakes. That is, do everything in moderation.

Don't visit a neighbour frequently; you may lose value.

Verse 17 exhorts to seldom set foot in your neighbour's house - too much of you, and he will hate you.

Do not repay evil for evil. - Verses 21-22. See also Romans 12:17-21. It is also worth noting: "Evil will never leave the house of one who pays back evil for good." - Proverbs 17:13

Avoid domestic quarrel (especially women).
Verse 24 states that it is better to live on a corner of the roof than share a house with a quarrelsome wife. Similar verses show up three more times in the book of proverbs (Proverbs 19:13, Proverbs 21:9, and Proverbs 27:15).

Moral Maxims 2

Proverbs 26

Like the previous chapter (Proverbs 25), this chapter teaches moral excellence as well. It also addresses in-depth behaviours showing lack of good sense or judgement and how you can guide against meddling in a quarrel or starting strife. Laziness is also addressed.

REGARDING A FOOL

A fool is someone who is lacking essential qualities in judgement, sense, or understanding. In Verses 1, 3-12, some observations of foolish behaviours and what you should not do when you are at the receiving end of such behaviours are expressed.

But how can you possibly reply to a fool when the need arises? Let us look at Matthew 16:1-4. The demand for a sign by the Pharisees and Sadducees prompted an answer from Jesus Christ that exposed their folly. Notice that Jesus did not hang around after replying to them: "Jesus then left them and went away."

When you regard or esteem a fool or give a fool a high or noble rank, it is not appropriate (verses 1 and 8). Imagine tying a stone to a catapult; you are more likely to injure yourself because the stone is going nowhere but back toward you. Essentially, the

Preacher is saying one should behave wisely.

UNDESERVED CURSE

In verse 2, a curse undeserved will not materialize. If you curse without a reason, it will return to you. See also Deuteronomy 23:5. More importantly, it is not good to curse anyone, for we are made in the likeness of God. See James 3:8-12.

Was Jacob's curse the cause of Rachel's death? Examine Genesis 31:19, 30-32, and Genesis 35:16-18.

THE LAZY MAN

Verses 13-16: Regarding work or a task, a lazy man or woman will always give an excuse; he or she is not inclined toward work or exertion (especially a strenuous effort). But the scriptures encourage working hard. Read 2 Thessalonians 3:10-11.

Studies of the scriptures show that everyone who was blessed with wealth was industrious. For example, Isaac dug several wells and sowed before he could reap (Genesis 26:12-28).

Despite reducing his wages ten times while with Laban, Jacob worked hard and God blessed him (Genesis 30:25-33).

> "It was like this for the twenty years I was in your household. I worked for you fourteen years for your two daughters and six years for your flocks, and **you changed my wages ten times.**"
>
> - Genesis 31:41

Can a lazy woman be a virtuous woman? Read Proverbs 31:10-30. You should not be lazy in praying either. Pray without ceasing. (Read 1 Thessalonians 5:17, Ephesians 6:18, and Luke 18:1, 7.)

DON'T STIR UP TROUBLE
Verse 17: Do not intrude into other people's affairs or business ...But make peace when you can.

Verses 18-19: Deception is considered similar to firebrand (a piece of wood that has been burned or is burning) or an arrow thrown by a madman. It is simply dangerous.

Verses 20 and 22: Don't be a talebearer.
Anyone who spreads malicious stories or gossip will always cause trouble. Avoid such people. Proverbs 20:19 recommends that you do not befriend a talebearer. To fully understand the effect talebearers have on a church, read 3 John 1:1-11.

Verses 23, 24, and 28 warn: Don't be deceived by flattering tongues.

MEASURE FOR MEASURE!
Verse 27: "If a man digs a pit, he will fall into it; if a man rolls a stone, it will roll back on him." This is evident in the case of Haman. He built the gallows to hang Mordecai, but he was hanged there instead. Read Esther 7:9-10.

See also Judges 1:6-7:

> "Adoni-Bezek fled, but they chased him and caught him, and cut off his thumbs and big toes. Then Adoni-Bezek said, 'Seventy kings with their thumbs and big toes cut off have picked up scraps under my table. Now God has paid me back for what I did to them.' They brought him to Jerusalem, and he died there."

Simply put, don't do evil.

Moral Maxims 3

Proverbs 27

"Now Daniel so distinguished himself among the administrators and the satraps by his exceptional qualities that the king planned to set him over the whole kingdom." - Daniel 6:3

If you want to acquire excellent spirit (exceptional qualities) and a place of respect in the society where you live, work, and worship, there are various virtues and observations that can impart beneficial knowledge into anyone who is willing to learn. They can be found in Proverbs and Ecclesiastes.

DO NOT BOAST

Verses 1 and 21 caution to never boast about anything, let alone about what lies ahead of you. Even when you have great accomplishments like that of David, be modest. 1 Samuel 18:7 reads:

"As they danced, they sang: 'Saul has slain his thousands, and David his tens of thousands.'"

This is what the Lord says:

"Let not the wise boast of their wisdom or the strong boast of their strength or the rich boast of their riches, 24but let the one who

boasts boast about this: that they have the understanding to know me, that I am the Lord, who exercises kindness, justice, and righteousness on earth, for in these I delight." - Jeremiah 9:23-24

When making plans for the future, "Commit your way to the Lord; trust in him and he will do this."- Psalm 37:5

LET OTHERS PRAISE YOU

Verse 2 is similar to verse 1. The scripture warns that we must (not be desirous of vain glory, provoking one another, or envying one another) - Galatians 5:26

Also see Proverbs 25:27 and 2 Corinthians 10:10-18.

CONTROL YOUR ANGER

Verse 3: Because a fool is someone who lacks essential qualities in sense, when angry, he or she loses control. If you cannot control your anger, you are like a city without walls: open to attack from any side. - Proverbs 25:28

JEALOUSY

Verse 4: One of the acts of the sinful nature is jealousy (Galatians 5:19-20). If you are jealous of others, you are not spiritual. Read 1 Corinthians 3:1-3. 1 Samuel 18:8 reads:

> *"Saul was very angry; this refrain displeased him greatly. 'They have credited David with tens of thousands,' he thought, 'but me with only thousands. What more can he get but the kingdom?'"*

STOP FLATTERING

Verses 5 and 9: It is better to say the truth openly than to conceal one's true feeling or intention. Read Proverbs 28:23 and Psalm 12:3.

DON'T BE DEVIOUS; DON'T BE A BETRAYER

Verse 6: When rightly corrected or advised by a friend, take it on board. With a deceitful kiss, Judas indicated Christ to the enemy. Read Psalm 141:5, Matthew 19:16-22, and Mark 14:44-46.

GIVE IN SECRET

Verse 14: "Be careful not to do your 'acts of righteousness' before men, to be seen by them. If you do, you will have no reward from your Father in heaven..." - Matthew 6:1-4.

NO CHOICE FOR A BEGGAR!

Verse 7: When the Prodigal Son spent all that he had, for lack of food, he ate the leftovers of the swine (Luke 15:16) ... and when you are full, you will refuse even something as sweet as honey.

BE FOCUSED

Verse 8: Do not wander about without a destination or purpose. 1 Timothy 5:13 reads,

> "Besides, they get into the habit of being idle and going about from house to house. And not only do they become idlers, but also gossips and busybodies, saying things they ought not to."

And, "If a man is lazy, the rafters sag; if his hands are idle, the house leaks."- Ecclesiastes 10:18

DO NOT FORSAKE FRIENDSHIP

Verse 10: Since there is a friend who sticks closer than a brother (Proverbs 18:24), do not forsake your friends. There are many benefits you can derive from friendship. Examine Jonathan's friendship with David (1 Samuel 18). Most importantly, your friend must be one who will help you find strength in God. 1 Samuel 23:16 reads:

> "And Saul's son Jonathan went to David at Horesh and helped him find strength in God."

However, when choosing friends, avoid talebearers (Proverbs 20:19) and angry people (Proverbs 22:24).

ON WISDOM

Verse 11: A wise son will make his father proud.
Verse 12: Wisdom gives life. (A prudent man is one who is wise in handling practical matters and who exercises good judgement or common sense). Read Ecclesiastes 7:12.
Verse 13: Don't be a surety for a stranger. If he or she defaults, where will you find him or her? It is stupidity.

WOMEN, AVOID NAGGING

Verses 15-16: A constant dripping on a rainy day will definitely halt or disturb some activities on such a day ... With a nagging wife, you will get the same and she cannot be contained. Listen to this: "Better to live on a corner of the roof than share a house with a quarrelsome wife." - Proverbs 25:24.

ASSOCIATE WITH WISE PEOPLE
Verse 17: Wise people, amongst other things, possess knowledge and discretion (Proverbs 8:12). Hanging around such people can make you understand things better.

YOUR DEEDS WILL BE REWARDED
Verse 18: Men's deed will not go unrewarded. Jeremiah 17:10 says, "I the LORD search the heart and examine the mind, to reward a man according to his conduct, according to what his deeds deserve." Read Esther 6:1-3.

A MAN'S HEART REFLECTS HIM
Verse 19: "Watch out! Be on your guard against all kinds of greed; life does not consist in an abundance of possessions." - Matthew 12:34-35

Verse 20: **THE MORE THINGS YOU ACQUIRE, THE LESS YOU ARE SATISFIED.** Read Ecclesiastes 2:4-10. Listen to this:

> "Then he said to them, 'Watch out! Be on your guard against all kinds of greed; a man's life does not consist in the abundance of his possessions.'" - Luke 12:15

BE THRIFTY

Verses 23-27: Give careful attention to your business; know your stock and the state of your finance. Why is stocktaking necessary? It is to know the accurate value of the stock held in a business.

Moral Maxims 4

Proverbs 28

Since the ancient days, there have been three kinds of people in the world: the high, the middle, and the low classes. Even the scripture made it known that there will be poor people in our midst (Deuteronomy 15:7), and rulers and kings will be made out of us. Lessons on moral excellence that are good for all classes of people will be found in the book of Proverbs. Oppression, one of the major causes of the downfall of kings, rulers, and people in positions of authority, is dealt with in this chapter. Note:

> "Your wickedness affects only a man like yourself, and your righteousness only the sons of men." - Job 35:8

GUILTY CONSCIENCE

Verses 1 and 17: People who do evil also have a sense of right and wrong; therefore, wicked people don't have peace of mind. They are always running for the fear of apprehension. As the wicked runs for his sins, the Lord also moves far from him. You are warned; don't support a murderer. See Proverbs 15:29.

ON REBELLION

Verses 2 and 25: Organized opposition toward a constituted

authority does not only destabilize. It also breeds many desirous rulers. And greedy people will stir up dissension (disagreement leading to a quarrel) so they can get a position or reward.

OPPRESSION

This subject is featured in five verses: 3, 12, 15, 16, and 28. People oppress with power or money (or both since money gives people power in certain communities). But the scripture warns:

> *"Do not take advantage of each other, but fear your God. I am the Lord your God."* - Leviticus 25:17

Do not take advantage of your fellow brethren, the Lord frowns at such. - Psalms 12:5

UPHOLD THE LAW

Verse 4: Those who keep the law will always have to contend with the wicked since there will be people approving the deeds of the wicked ones. Read Romans 1:32 and Proverbs 19:6.

EVIL MEN DO NOT UNDERSTAND GOD'S JUDGEMENT

Verse 5: Since the wicked people do not have the spirit of God in them, they also do not understand the judgement of God. Didn't the scripture say, "Understanding is a fountain of life to those who have it, but folly brings punishment to fools"? (Proverbs 16:22). Read Psalm 92:6-7.

WEALTH MAY MAKE YOUR WAY PERVERSE

Verses 6 and 11: Money may be the answer for everything (Ecclesiastes 10:19), but it won't buy knowledge, wisdom, and understanding that is of God. A poor wisely behaved man is better than a rich man whose behaviour is contrary to good sense. Read Proverbs 11:28.

A GOOD CHILD IS THE PRIDE OF THE FATHER

Verses 7 and 24: A child having or showing good taste or judgement will delight the parents. It is wickedness to defraud your parents. Parents have an obligation to instruct and correct their children. Also note that "...parents are the pride of their children" (Proverbs 17:6). Read Proverbs 23:24-25.

ILL-GOTTEN WEALTH

Verses 8 and 20-22: If you are aspiring to become rich, there are a few things you need to know. Listen to this:

> "People who want to get rich fall into temptation and a trap and into many foolish and harmful desires that plunge men into ruin and destruction." - 1 Timothy 6:9

And if you are already comfortable, you ought to be careful (1 Timothy 6:17). See Ecclesiastes 2:26 and 1 Timothy 6:10. Proverbs 21:5 reads,

> "The plans of the diligent lead to profit as surely as haste leads to poverty."

And Proverbs 13:11 says:

> "Dishonest money dwindles away, but he who gathers money little by little makes it grow."

HEED INSTRUCTIONS
Verse 9: Since the Lord is far from the wicked (Proverbs 15:29), he detests the sacrifice of the wicked, he detests the way of the wicked (Proverbs 15:8-9), and the prayers of a wicked person are detestable. Read Isaiah 1:12-16.

DON'T MISLEAD ANYONE
Verse 10 simply means that you must not mislead anyone.

CONFESS YOUR SINS
Verse 13: Confession precedes forgiveness; therefore, it is essential to confess to:
(1) God our sins
(2) Our neighbour the wrong(s) that we may have done

God will forgive those who confess their sins and are repentant. Read Psalm 32:3-5 and Psalm 66:18.
James 5:16 says:

> "Therefore confess your sins to each other and pray for each other so that you may be healed. The prayer of a righteous man is powerful and effective."

DON'T HARDEN YOUR HEART

Verse 14: Showing respect to God is good, but if you do not take to correction, you will fall into trouble.

REBUKE RATHER THAN FLATTER

Verse 23: It is better to wisely criticize or reprimand somebody than to flatter.

WARNING AGAINST LAZINESS

Verse 19 is simply a warning to people who are lazy. Read Proverbs 6:9-11 and 18:9.

A lazy person is one who:
- puts off starting what he/she should do,
- does not finish what he/she started, and/or
- when faced with a difficult task gives excuses instead of looking for solutions.

BE GENEROUS

Verse 27: The scriptures warned against withholding from doing good. James 4:17 reads:

> "Anyone, then, who knows the good he ought to do and doesn't do it, sins."

To understand more about giving to the poor, please read Deuteronomy 15:7-11.

Moral Maxims 5

Proverbs 29

This is the last of the five chapters dealing with moral excellence and observations I have chosen to discuss. It concludes that when your way is right before God, you will be hated with disgust by people who are unjust (Verses 9 and 27). The question is: How would you handle situations where you find you have been hated because of your uprightness and good deeds? Although you have the wisdom of God in you, you are likely to make a mistake.

Again, this chapter highlights why it is essential to acquire wisdom. It is also good to note that with humility comes wisdom (Proverbs 11:2).

Ecclesiastes 7:12 says,

> "Wisdom is a shelter as money is a shelter, but the advantage of knowledge is this: that wisdom preserves the life of its possessor."

If you have been counted worthy to lead or you are aspiring to be a leader, there are lessons in this chapter that can help to establish your authority.

HEED CORRECTION

Verse 1: Do not refuse correction. "Blessed is the man whom God corrects; so do not despise the discipline of the Almighty" (Job 5:17). Also read 2 Chronicles 36:15-16.

ON LEADERSHIP

Verses 2, 4, 12, 14, and 16.

Leaders and rulers must have these qualities:
1. They must rule with the fear of God.
2. They must not listen to lies.
3. They must be impartial in judgement.
4. They must not take a bribe.

Deuteronomy 16:19 reads,

> "Do not pervert justice or show partiality. Do not accept a bribe, for a bribe blinds the eyes of the wise and twists the words of the innocent."

See also Ecclesiastes 7:7.

Relations of rulers and leaders must ensure that they do not abuse authority or take advantage of the same. For example, Samuel's sons were dishonest and accepted bribes to give unfair decisions (1 Samuel 8:1-3). Also, what authority had Jezebel? She even killed the Lord's prophets and encouraged Ahab, her husband, to take Naboth's vineyard.

ON WISDOM

Verses 3, 11, and 20: Please read chapter 27 of this book.

Verse 8: Those who treat people with contempt (as inferior or worthless) will bring uproar to a city, but those who have wisdom will turn away anger. A lesson for leaders and rulers.

Verse 9: If you are wise, don't argue with a fool. Note:

> "Fools enjoy doing wrong, but anyone with good sense enjoys acting wisely." - Proverbs 10:23

IT IS DANGEROUS TO FLATTER

Verse 5: When you compliment insincerely, it is not good. Psalms 12:3 says, "Won't you chop off all flattering tongues that brag so loudly?"

ON WICKEDNESS

Verses 6 and 7: A wicked man will continue to sin and oppress. But God's commandment in Leviticus 25:17 forbids oppression.

ON PARENTING

Verses 15, 17, 19, and 21: Correct your child because: "Folly is bound up in the heart of a child, but the rod of discipline will drive it far away." - Proverbs 22:15

Also, don't pamper[c] a servant and correct your servant the same way you would your son.

c) **Pamper** *means to treat with excessive indulgence.*

TRUST IN GOD

Verse 25: Consider this statement:

> 'This is what the Lord says:
> "Cursed is the one who trusts in man, who draws strength from mere flesh and whose heart turns away from the Lord. ⁶ That person will be like a bush in the wastelands; they will not see prosperity when it comes. They will dwell in the parched places of the desert, in a salt land where no one lives. ⁷ "But blessed is the one who trusts in the Lord, whose confidence is in him..."'
>
> - Jeremiah 17:5-9

PROPHECY AS A GUIDE

Verse 18: Without vision people will be destroyed.

Warnings, instructions, and replies to our inquiries from the Lord sometimes come through prophecies. Imagine what would happen if God no longer talked to us. It happened to Saul. Read 1 Samuel 28:6. Look at 1 Samuel 3:1. (Visions were rare in those days.)

ON ANGER

Verse 22: A man's anger will cause him to sin. "For man's anger does not bring about the righteous life that God desires" (James 1:20). See also Matthew 5:22.

HUMILITY WILL BRING YOU HONOR

Verse 23: See 1 Peter 5:5-6.

DON'T BE FRIEND TO A THIEF

Verse 24: Let us view it in two ways: the curse on a thief is not a causeless curse; hence, it will stick. If you take an oath to say the truth and you say nothing, you are in danger. If you testify against your friend who is a thief, you are also in danger. Which way then? I would say it is better not to befriend a thief.

People you should not befriend were pointed out in the last five chapters:
1. A thief
2. A talebearer
3. An angry person

Should a lazy man or woman be added to the list above? You can add to the list above if you read 2 Timothy 3:1-5, 2 Thessalonians 3:6, and Romans 16:17.

> "Do not be misled: 'Bad company corrupts good character.'"
> - 1 Corinthians 15:33

A Virtuous Woman

The study of Proverbs 25-29 indicates certain behaviours women should avoid. For example, jealousy, nagging, etc. Some of these verses stimulate discussion of 'a virtuous woman' followed by, as you might guess, the discussion of 'a good husband'.

Looking at the whole of Proverbs 31, if the values there were taught to King Lemuel by a man, would the chapter have a different meaning today? If it were not a prophecy, how would it have been perceived? The 21st century woman should understand that the attributes of a virtuous woman in Proverbs 31 were taught by a woman (also a mother). Are these qualities acquirable?

To be a virtuous woman, you need to have the wisdom of God. This is evident in Proverbs 31:26.

Proverbs 14:1 reads:

> "The wise woman builds her house, but with her own hands the foolish one tears hers down."

And:

> "Folly is an unruly woman; she is simple and knows nothing..."
>
> - Proverbs 9:13-15

Looking through Proverbs 31:10-28, a virtuous woman is one who will take care of herself, her husband, her children, and the home.

THE MONETARY VALUE OF A VIRTUOUS WOMAN

Verse 10: How much would you pay to have a woman who is prudent, generous, honourable, and of high moral character? She is priceless.

If a man cannot buy a wife of noble character, how can he get one? Before answering the question, look at the verse below:

> "Houses and wealth are inherited from parents, but **a prudent wife is from the LORD.**" - Proverbs 19:14

Anyone seeking a good wife should pray to God for one. That is, put your request before the Lord, trust in him, wait on him, and he will do what you require of him. If you marry a woman because of her beauty, what will happen if that beauty suddenly fades? If you marry a woman because of her wealth, what will happen should her wealth dwindle? If you marry a woman because of her social status, will you still be together if she's no longer relevant in society? If you rush into marriage, are you prepared for the surprises? Reliance on God for a good wife or husband means nothing will catch you unaware.

With reference to Proverbs 31, the following are the attributes of a virtuous woman.

SHE IS GOOD TO HER HUSBAND

Verse 12: She understands that she should love her husband and fulfill her marital duties.

> "The husband should fulfill his marital duty to his wife, and likewise the wife to her husband. The wife's body does not belong to her alone but also to her husband. In the same way, the husband's body does not belong to him alone but also to his wife."
> - 1 Corinthians 7:3-4

She is kind to her husband.

> "She brings him good, not harm, all the days of her life."
> - Proverbs 31:12

She is submissive to her husband. Ephesians 5:22-24 reads:

> "Wives, submit yourselves unto your own husbands, as unto the Lord. ...Therefore as the church is subject unto Christ, so let the wives be to their own husbands in everything."

See also 1 Peter 3:1.

SHE IS A HOME KEEPER

Verses 15, 21, 22, and 27: One good attribute tends to give rise to another. She looks after her husband and his interests.

A woman who wants to attain the noble standard should look at Titus 2:4:

> *"'That they may teach the young women to be sober, to love their husbands, to love their children, To be discreet[d], chaste[e], keepers at home, good, obedient to their own husbands, that the word of God be not blasphemed.' ...And she's not a drunkard."*

d) **Discreet** means showing prudence and wise self-restraint in speech and behaviour.

e) **Chaste** means morally pure in thought or conduct; decent and modest.

SHE IS A GOOD MOTHER

Verses 15 and 26: Not only will she love her children, she will impress God's laws on them and teach them as instructed in Deuteronomy 6:6-9.

SHE IS NOT LAZY

Verses 13, 15, 17, and 19: Anyone who is lazy cannot build. One of the attributes of a virtuous woman is that she's not opposed to hard work. She's hardly a busybody. Read 2 Thessalonians 3:11-12.

SHE IS GENEROUS

Verse 20: Apart from being good to her family, her generosity extends to the poor and needy.

SHE IS PRUDENT

Verses 16 and 18: When dealing with matters regarding money, she exercises good judgement; she is a wise spender.

SHE IS ALSO SKILLFUL

Verses 19, 22, and 24: She is a woman who undertakes her work with perseverance and care. She looks after herself well and is not scruffy.

SHE IS HONOURABLE

Verses 23, 25, 28, and 29: She is a highly esteemed woman and one who brings honour to her husband. The result of exhibiting the invaluable attributes listed above will make her husband have full confidence in her (verse 11). A man at peace at home will think right. Can we say the same of the husband of a nagging woman? He is probably sheltered on the roof top as you are reading this book.

AND WHAT DOES SHE GET FOR ALL OF THESE?

Praises upon praises. Imagine waking up every morning to commendations or admirations by your husband and/or children; it is enough to fuel the rest of the day's activities.

> "Her children arise and call her blessed; her husband also, and he praises her." - Proverbs 31:28

She will laugh in the future (Proverbs 31:25). See the blessing pronounced on Ruth, Boaz's wife, in Ruth 4:11-12.

Show me a king who would not proudly wear his crown.

> *"A wife of noble character is her husband's crown, but a disgraceful wife is like decay in his bones."* - Proverbs 12:4

Are there examples of virtuous women in the bible? Discuss.

A Good Husband

Great as our God is, he sometimes describe himself as a 'husband' when speaking in parable.

> "For your Maker is your husband - the Lord Almighty is his name - the Holy One of Israel is your Redeemer; he is called the God of all the earth." - Isaiah 54:5

The comparison made in Ephesians 5:23 defines the position of the husband as the head of the wife:

> "For the husband is the head of the wife as Christ is the head of the church, his body, of which he is the Savior."

ON LEADERSHIP

As the head, a good husband is expected to provide, amongst other things, spiritual leadership at home. These duties include:
- Taking his wife and children to church with him
- Teaching the scriptures
- Praying and fasting for the family regularly
- Conducting regular family devotions

These tasks are made easy if the wife is submissive. Read Ephesians 5:22. The scripture encourages husband and wife to devote time for prayers (1 Corinthians 7:5). Also look at Deuteronomy 6:6-9 on how to teach the children.

In other areas, a good husband will lead in a diligent manner.

ON LOVE

A good husband must love his wife (Ephesians 5:28). What is love? Examine these verses:

> *"Love is **patient**, love is **kind**. It does not **envy**, it does not **boast**, it is not **proud**. It is not **rude**, it is not **self-seeking**, it is not easily angered, it **keeps no record of wrongs**. Love does not **delight in evil** but rejoices with the truth. It always **protects**, always **trusts**, always **hopes**, always **perseveres**." - 1 Corinthians 13:4-7*

Look at the keywords in bold, more than a dozen of them. Add another to the list above; *love will **communicate**.*

It is important for a good husband to love his wife. Listen to this:

> *"Husbands, in the same way be considerate as you live with your wives, and treat them with respect as the weaker partner and as heirs with you of the gracious gift of life, so that nothing will hinder your prayers." - 1 Peter 3:7*

MARITAL DUTY

A good husband will fulfill his marital duty. Look at the advice of Apostle Paul in 1 Corinthians 7:3-5:

> "The husband should fulfill his marital duty to his wife, and likewise the wife to her husband. The wife's body does not belong to her alone but also to her husband. In the same way, the husband's body does not belong to him alone but also to his wife. Do not deprive each other except by mutual consent and for a time, so that you may devote yourselves to prayer. Then come together again so that Satan will not tempt you because of your lack of self-control."

You will notice that the issue of temptation that can arise from not fulfilling marital duty or denial is highlighted in the statement above.

WILL BE RESPONSIBLE

If a virtuous woman is said to provide food for her family (Proverbs 31:15), as the head of the family, a good husband should do more: look after his family. In a situation where a wife earns more than her husband or the husband is not gainfully employed, common sense should apply. Look at 1 Timothy 5:8:

> "If anyone does not provide for his relatives, and especially for his immediate family, he has denied the faith and is worse than an unbeliever."

LIVE JOYFULLY

"A joyful heart makes a cheerful face, but when the heart is sad, the spirit is broken" (Proverbs 15:13). Going by what the scripture says, a good husband will learn how to enjoy life with his wife. He will know what gladdens his wife's heart. You are encouraged below:

> "Enjoy life with your wife, whom you love, all the days of this meaningless life that God has given you under the sun - all your meaningless days. For this is your lot in life and in your toilsome labor under the sun." - Ecclesiastes 9:9

There are four simple rules in Colossians 3:18-21 for the Christian households. Two of them are addressed to men.

1. Wives, submit to your husbands, as is fitting in the Lord.
2. **Husbands, love your wives and do not be harsh with them.**
3. Children, obey your parents in everything, for this pleases the Lord.
4. **Fathers, do not embitter your children**, or they will become discouraged.

FORNICATION AND ADULTERY

Adultery often interferes with marital relations. Can a man who indulges in fornication or adultery be a good husband? Discuss this to hear opinions. Consider all the salient perils and health issues. Any man wishing to be a good husband should pray against sexual immoralities because

> "Many are the victims she has brought down; her slain are a mighty throng. [27] Her house is a highway to the grave, leading down to the chambers of death." - Proverbs 7:26-27

Jealousy

Anger is cruel and fury overwhelming, but who can stand before jealousy?
- Proverbs 27:4

The importance of this topic is seen in the underlined sentence of the following bible quotation:

> "The acts of the sinful nature are obvious: sexual immorality, impurity, and debauchery; idolatry and witchcraft; hatred, discord, jealousy, fits of rage, selfish ambition, dissensions, factions, and envy; drunkenness, orgies, and the like. <u>I warn you, as I did before, that those who live like this will not inherit the Kingdom of God.</u>"
> *- Galatians 5:20-21*

Also read Romans 13:13 and 1 Corinthians 3:3.

Jealousy, an attitude stemming from the feelings of envy or bitterness, is often dangerous and, if not dealt with, will make you sin.

This topic seeks to address jealousy arising from the success of others, the possessions of others, or the status of others and not from the fear of being displaced by a rival in a romantic relationship. Don't be disappointed.

How do you become jealous or how does jealousy come about?

Jealousy may come about as a result of:
1. Low self-esteem
2. Underachievement
3. Hatred
4. Failure
5. Selfishness
6. Greed
7. Favouritism
8. Overpraising or over-pampering one child over another

Parents will do well by ensuring each child gets proper career counseling. I was good in mathematics but my junior brother was poor in mathematics. However, he had first-class honours in fine arts and design. During our secondary school education, he was expected to do as well as I did in numeracy. Expecting one child to do as well as another academically may result in jealousy amongst sibling (i.e. sibling rivalry).

What are the effects of jealousy?

The effects of jealousy are many, if not controlled. The ultimate is death. However, one can expect to see or feel: hatred, malice, bullying, insubordination, anger, strife, sabotage, opposition, witch-hunting, cruelty, and destruction (like arson).

In a church environment, jealousy can hinder growth. A pastor or shepherd being jealous of the gift(s) of the Holy Spirit in members will not allow such gifts to thrive. Members who are jealous of the gifts of others will not allow good growth. Look at how Moses dealt with Joshua's outburst in Numbers 11:24-29. This is a lesson for all aides and personal assistants to pastors, prophets, and general overseers.

How can you overcome jealousy?
Jealousy is an evil spirit, and like any other evil spirit, it can be banished by fervent prayers.

When teamwork is required, work as part of a team.

Take a look at Philippians 2:3:

> *"Do nothing out of selfish ambition or vain conceit, but in humility consider others better than yourselves."*

If you do not have the ability, skill, spiritual gift, and/or possession you desire to have, pray for it/them. Also study and train to develop your skills.

On Sibling Rivalry
Do not give special treatment to one sibling and ignore another. Nonetheless, achievements and good behaviour should be rewarded. Do not compare siblings; get proper career counseling to know each one's abilities (especially academic).

Discuss the examples below:

Saul versus David:

Read 1 Samuel 18. (Consider the age difference.) Jonathan, Saul's son, was David's friend. Saul was old enough to be David's father, but he hated him. Older people can be jealous of younger people's status or achievements.

Korah, Dathan, and Abiram versus Moses:

Read Numbers 16. (Moses' status and spiritual ability were factors here.) What about Miriam opposing Moses?

Paul and Silas' experience:

Read Acts 13:42-45. In verse 44, you will notice that Paul first preached in the synagogue, and on the following Sabbath day, he was speaking to almost the whole city.

> *"When the Jews saw the crowds, they were filled with jealousy and talked abusively against what Paul was saying."* - Acts 13:45

Sanballat and Tobiah opposed rebuilding the walls of Jerusalem.
Was opposition born out of jealousy? Read Nehemiah 4.

Cain and Abel's offerings - Genesis 4.

Can jealous people compete healthily?

Revenge

To inflict punishment in return for (injury or insult); a retaliatory measure

Following the Ten Commandments, God, through Moses, set several judgements before his people in Exodus 21 and 22. It was a way of making sure that the people led by Moses did not take law into their own hands. These judgements were imposed, and to prevent retributive justice, the Lord instructed further in Leviticus 19:18 thusly:

> "Do not seek revenge or bear a grudge against one of your people, but love your neighbour as yourself. I am the Lord."

But instructions like those found in Deuteronomy 23:3-6 should in no way encourage us toward revenge. See Ezekiel 25:12-15. If you have been wronged, listen to this:

> "Repay no one evil for evil, but take thought for what is noble in the sight of all. [18] If possible, so far as it depends upon you, live peaceably with all. [19] Beloved, never avenge yourselves, but leave it to the wrath of God; for it is written, 'Vengeance is mine, I will repay,' says the Lord. [20] No, 'if your enemy is hungry, feed him; if he is thirsty, give him drink; for by so doing you will heap burning coals upon his head. [21] Do not be overcome by evil, but overcome evil with good." - Romans 12:17-21

WHAT SPURS REVENGE?
1. Inability to forgive
2. Lack of knowledge of the scriptures/wisdom
3. Lack of love
4. Lifelong hatred
5. Power / Money / Influence
6. Repeated anger
7. Cheating

EXAMPLES OF INSTANCES OF REVENGE

Revenge for Dinah

When Shechem raped Dinah, the daughter of Jacob, Simeon and Levi (sons of Jacob) killed Shechem and his father and all the males in the city. Read Genesis 34:1-2 and 25-27. Simeon and Levi's action troubled Jacob, and God instructed him to move from that city. In Jacob's last words, Simeon and Levi were cursed (Genesis 49:5-7). One would ask: Does the punishment fit the crime?

Joab killed Abner in retaliation for Asahel's death.

> "Now when Abner returned to Hebron, Joab took him aside into an inner chamber, as if to speak with him privately. And there, to avenge the blood of his brother Asahel, Joab stabbed him in the stomach, and he died..." - 2 Samuel 3:27-30

Here, Joab killed at peacetime. Look at David's instruction to Solomon regarding Joab's action in 1 Kings 2:5-6. The story began in 2 Samuel 2:18-23 where Abner struck down Asahel.

The Gibeonites sought revenge for Saul's misdeeds.

Saul violated the treaty between the Gibeonites and Israel. One thing led to another and a revenge for his action was sought long after his death. True! *"The evil that men do lives after them..."* Read Joshua 9:1-15 and 2 Samuel 21:1-9. Was this the act of God or lifelong hatred?

EXERCISING RESTRAINT TO PREVENT REVENGE

There are a few examples to point to in the bible regarding the show of restraint to prevent revenge. When Nabal insulted David, he exercised restraint by heeding Abigail's advice. See 1 Samuel 25:1-39.

David showed restraint by not killing Saul. Read 1 Samuel 19:1-2 and 1 Samuel 24:1-7. Amazing! See the wise conclusion of Saul in 1 Samuel 24:19-20. When your ways please the Lord, even your enemy will be at peace with you. In 1 Samuel 24:20, Saul said to David, "I know that you will surely be king..."

> *"I know that you will surely be king and that the kingdom of Israel will be established in your hands."*

Jesus versus the Accusers: As they crucified him, he said:

> *"Father, forgive them, for they do not know what they are doing." And they divided up his clothes by casting lots."* - Luke 23:34

In the above examples involving David, the Lord ordered his steps and Psalm 119:133 says:

> "*Direct my footsteps according to your word; let no sin rule over me.*"

Let these words guide you:
> "*You have heard that it was said, 'Eye for eye, and tooth for tooth.' [39]But I tell you, do not resist an evil person. If someone strikes you on the right cheek, turn to him the other also. [40]And if someone wants to sue you and take your tunic, let him have your cloak as well. [41]If someone forces you to go one mile, go with him two miles. [42]Give to the one who asks you, and do not turn away from the one who wants to borrow from you.*" - Matthew 5:38-42

DO NOT REPAY EVIL FOR GOOD

Taking revenge could have a lifelong consequence if you get it wrong (i.e., if the person whom you thought did wrong is guiltless).

> "*If a man pays back evil for good, evil will never leave his house.*"
> - Proverbs 17:13

Look at **David's charge to Solomon** in 1 Kings 2:5-9. David instructed Solomon to kill Joab and Shimei. Examine these verses (1 Kings 2:5-8, 28-46) to determine if Solomon's action was revenge or preventive action.

Is There Punishment for Our Sins?

Imagine that we have to live without any set rules. Having a set of rules without enforcement is like having no rules at all. With God, there are various ways in which he enforces his laws and commandments. Discuss laws concerning protection of property, social responsibility, and personal injuries in Exodus 22 and 23. Are they relevant today?

There are times when people feel that they are above the law. There were times like that in those days too. Judges 17:6 says, "In those days there was no king in Israel, but every man did that which was right in his own eyes." See also Judges 21:25.

God is no respecter of persons. If he were, imagine what people would have gotten or will get away with. Various ways in which God will punish disobedience can be seen in Leviticus 26:14-39. See also 1 Chronicles 21:1-13. It is evident in the following verses that there is punishment for sins: Genesis 4:8-13, Isaiah 53:5, and Ezra 9:13.

That there is punishment for our sins is made clear in Hosea 9:7:

> "The days of punishment are coming, the days of reckoning are at hand. Let Israel know this. Because your sins are so many and your hostility so great, the prophet is considered a fool, the inspired man a maniac."

That Christ bore the marks of our sins does not mean we have the freedom or grace to continue to disobey God. What then? Shall we sin because we are not under law but under grace? By no means! - Romans 6:15. See also Hebrews 6:6.

Transferred Punishment!

Regarding punishment, God made clear a course of action he would follow: punishing generations after the offender.

> "...maintaining love to thousands, and forgiving wickedness, rebellion, and sin. Yet he does not leave the guilty unpunished; he punishes the children and their children for the sin of the parents to the third and fourth generation." - Exodus 34:7

Let us look at the following references.
Jeremiah 32:18:
> "You show love to thousands but bring the punishment for the fathers' sins into the laps of their children after them. O great and powerful God, whose name is the Lord Almighty..."

Lamentations 5:7:
> "Our fathers sinned and are no more, and we bear their punishment."

Seven descendants of King Saul were killed for a sin they knew nothing about. Read 2 Samuel 21:1-7. If you are pondering *"Why does God do this?"* Job also pondered the same. He wanted God to repay the wicked so that they themselves would experience it. Read Job 21:17-22.

Parents must understand that their bad deeds can affect their children even long after their death. There is the need to reflect on the likely consequences of our behaviour, action, or deeds.

Can the righteous share in the punishment of the wicked? Remember this: that by one man's sin many were made sinners (Romans 5:17-19).

When do we sin?
It is not only when we do contrary to the Ten Commandments that we sin. We sin when we know what is right or good and don't do it. See James 4:17, Deuteronomy 15:9, and 2 Chronicles 32:25.

Measure for Measure
When David killed Uriah (2 Samuel 12), look at what David prescribed as punishment (in verses 5-6). Then look at what God said in verses 10 and 11. Adoni-Bezek had his thumb cut as he did to others. - Judges 1:4-7

On God's Mercy

God's mercy comes with repentance. Read 2 Peter 3:9: "...He is patient with you, not wanting anyone to perish, but everyone to come to repentance." See also Luke 3:8. What a merciful God we serve. In Isaiah 1:18 he said, *"Come now, let us reason together..."*

Micah 7:18 reads,

> *"Who is a God like you, who pardons sin and forgives the transgression of the remnant of his inheritance? You do not stay angry forever but delight to show mercy."*

Isaiah 55:7 says,

> *Let the wicked forsake his way, and the unrighteous man his thoughts: and let him return unto the Lord, and he will have mercy upon him; and to our God, for he will abundantly pardon.*

On Judgement

Christ will return to judge us and this is what he will do:

> "He will punish those who do not know God and do not obey the gospel of our Lord Jesus. They will be punished with everlasting destruction and shut out from the presence of the Lord and from the glory of his might on the day he comes to be glorified in his holy people and to be marveled at among all those who have believed."
>
> — 2 Thessalonians 1:8-10

The Grace of Giving

Imagine this: You are comfortable, you don't steal, you do not commit adultery, and no one will hear you give a false testimony, but to have treasure in heaven, you will need to sell your possessions and give to the poor (Matthew 19:16-22). How would you feel? Also read Luke 12:33.

Avoidance of sin is pleasing to God, but perfection is attained when you look after the poor and needy. Throughout the scriptures, the act of giving is encouraged while withholding more than necessary is disapproved of. Look at the parable of the Sheep and the Goats in Matthew 25:31-46. Listen to this:

> "One man gives freely, yet gains even more; another withholds unduly, but comes to poverty. A generous man will prosper; he who refreshes others will himself be refreshed. People curse the man who hoards grain, but blessing crowns him who is willing to sell."
>
> - Proverbs 11:24-26

DO NOT BE TIGHTFISTED

When you are blessed, be open-handed and give freely. Otherwise, it could be counted as sin if you are hardhearted. Read Deuteronomy 15:7-11 to find out about this. And Proverbs 3:27 says:

> *"Withhold not good from them to whom it is due, when it is in the power of thine hand to do it."*

THE GOOD SAMARITAN
Look at Luke 10:30-37.

SOW GENEROUSLY
Look at 2 Corinthians 9:6-15 and Acts 4:32-35. The effect of sowing generously can be seen in the two references above. Sometimes some Christians find it very difficult to give, but there must be reasons why the scriptures encourage us to give generously to the poor and needy.

WHAT YOU GET FOR GIVING
Giving generously opens the way to blessing.
> *"A gift opens the way and ushers the giver into the presence of the great."* - Proverbs 18:16

A blessing was pronounced on the Widow at Zarephath by Elijah for her generosity (1 Kings 17:14). The act of generosity was a result of the instructions from Elijah, but there is a blessing for obedience as well. Did God intentionally bless this woman? Read Luke 4:25-27.

- You will be made rich in every way.
    > *"...so that you can be generous on every occasion, and ... your generosity will result in thanksgiving to God."* - 2 Corinthians 9:11

- God will bless you in all your works and in everything you put your hand to.

    "Give generously to Him and do so without a grudging heart; then because of this the Lord your God will bless you in all your work and in everything you put your hand to." - Deuteronomy 15:10

- You will be honoured and encouraged to do more.

    "...their horn will be lifted high in honour." - Psalm 112:9

- Your generosity to others can have an effect that is similar to this:

    "...And God's grace was so powerfully at work in them all that there were no needy persons among them..." - Acts 4:33-34

- Your alms will become a memorial offering before God. Read Acts 10:1-7.

- If the act of generosity is showing love, then it is part of fulfillment of the Law. Read Luke 10:26-28 and Hebrews 13:16.

Can the act of generosity prolong life? Discuss Acts 9:34-42.

FINISH THE WORK

When you begin an act of generosity, endeavour to finish it. Imagine giving a hungry man who has no oven a half-baked loaf of bread. Why whet the poor man's appetite? Read 2 Corinthians 8:8-15.

GIVE IN SECRET

The instructions in Matthew 6:1-4 are clear. Look at this news brief from April 2009 following the economic meltdown:

"Not everyone is willing to take credit for their good deeds: In recent weeks, at least nine American universities have received donations of well more than $1 million each from anonymous donors, the Associated Press reported. The donations ranged in size from $1.5 million for the University of North Carolina-Asheville to $8 million for Purdue University in Indiana."

Story link: http://abcnews.go.com/business/Economy/story?id=7363706&page=1

For their generosity, these people were referred to as *Recession Angels*.

IS GENEROSITY ABOUT GIVING MONEY?

Other than money, giving can occur in the following ways:
- Giving in kind - goods and services.
- Voluntary service to non-profit organizations
- Giving assistance to people or a person

WHO DO YOU GIVE TO?
- The poor and needy
- God's service, including the servants of God
- Your parents
- Strangers

> "Do not forget to show hospitality to strangers, for by so doing some people have shown hospitality to angels without knowing it."
> — Hebrews 13:2

BUT BE CAREFUL...

> "One who oppresses the poor to increase his wealth and one who gives gifts to the rich - both come to poverty." - Proverbs 22:16

Discuss the generosity of the Widow at Zarephath in 1 Kings 17:7-15. Was Elijah poor or needy?

The Enemy's Tactics

Everyone has a season of respite. Jesus Christ had one shortly after his encounter with the devil in Luke 4:13:

> "And when the devil had ended all the temptation, he departed from him for a season."

Followers of Christ are expected to experience similar, that is, have a season of respite (a short interval of rest or relief). The question is: *When does this respite end?* During Christ's season of respite, he continued to teach in the synagogues, and he later withdrew to pray in the wilderness (Luke 5:16). But the scripture warned that we: "Be alert and of sober mind. Your enemy the devil prowls around like a roaring lion looking for someone to devour." - 1 Peter 5:8

Let us look at what a lion would do to get its prey. First, it soundlessly stalks the prey. The next thing is to try and separate its prey from a herd and bring it down. If the prey is alone, the job is easier. If you are a Christian, the first thing the enemy will try to do is to separate you from Christ. This can be gradual or it may suddenly happen. Look at Romans 8:35:

> "Who, then, can separate us from the love of Christ? Can trouble do it, or hardship or persecution or hunger or poverty or danger or death?"

Now, any of the following may separate you from the love of Christ: trouble, hardship, persecution, hunger, poverty, danger, unanswered prayer, or death. But you need to understand that:

> "For it has been granted to you on behalf of Christ not only to believe in him, but also to suffer for him." - Philippians 1:29

Romans 8:17 reads:

> "Now if we are children, then we are heirs - heirs of God and co-heirs with Christ, if indeed we share in his sufferings in order that we may also share in his glory."

Read Romans 5:3, 1 Peter 3:13-14, and 1 Peter 4:16-19.
There is no need to move away from Christ or stop going to church when we are tried, "Because he himself suffered when he was tempted, he is able to help those who are being tempted" (Hebrews 2:18). If the enemy does not succeed in stopping you from worshiping God, he will try to make you disobey God so that you will be denied the promised blessing and victory. Remember that the devil is cunning.

COMPLACENCY

This is not a strategy but rather a reminder that there is a period when you are most likely to be attacked. It is when you are feeling contentment or self-satisfaction. That is, when things in your life are hunky-dory. Look at the deeds of Amaziah, the King of Judah in 2 Chronicles 25 and the wickedness of King Joash (2

Kings 12:18-20 and 2 Chronicles 24:17-25). What ways did the enemy use in pulling them down? Now read Deuteronomy 8:11-18.

LAZINESS

The advice in Ephesians 6:18 is to pray without ceasing. No wonder one of the devil's tactics is to find ways of discouraging us from praying. How does this happen? Discuss this topic to hear different views. A common thing that happens to Christians is falling asleep just when they are about to pray or when praying. Read Colossians 4:2.

For more on how laziness may affect prosperity, see the parable of the Talents in Matthew 25:14-30. You will notice that the man who was given one talent was described as a *"lazy servant."*

DISCORD

To hinder prayer, the enemy can sow discord (lack of agreement among persons or groups). Read 1 Peter 3:7. The enemy knows that:

> *"...The prayer of a righteous person is powerful and effective."*
>
> - James 5:16

Note that the apostles were in one accord and their prayers were powerful and effective:

> *"They all joined together constantly in prayer, along with the women and Mary the mother of Jesus, and with his brothers."* - Acts 1:14

When you are not in agreement, you cannot pray together. Some couples may have experienced this situation, and it is important to always *settle disputes quickly* so that they do not stop you from praying and so that when you do pray, your prayers are not hindered.

FEAR

Amongst other things, the enemy uses fear to deter progress or deny us victory. When Saul and all of Israel heard of Goliath's threats, for forty days they were dismayed and greatly afraid (1 Samuel 17:10). David, a brave young man who had faith in God, defeated Goliath.

Regarding the spies sent out by Moses to explore the land of Canaan, Joshua and Caleb gave a good account while ten other spies were afraid of the giants they saw in that land. Read Numbers 13:30-33, Deuteronomy 20:1-4, 1 Chronicles 22:13, and 2 Chronicles 20:15 (...for the battle is not yours, but God's). The ten who were afraid got no reward.

Look at how the enemies set out to discourage the people of Judah. They hired people to make them afraid of going on building the temple of God (Ezra 4:1-5). The enemies also discouraged Nehemiah when he was rebuilding the walls of Jerusalem (Nehemiah 4). As soon as the plan of the enemy was known to them, this action followed:

> "But we prayed to our God and posted a guard day and night to meet this threat." - Nehemiah 4:9

A second attempt was made but it was not successful (Nehemiah 6:10-13). Even when your project is in support of the work of God (church building or charitable), you still need to pray to God for a successful completion and against hindrances. You will notice that in the two rebuilding projects, the builders were of one accord, unlike the builders of the Tower of Babel. How often are projects stifled by one or more of the enemy's tactics?

DOUBT

When you need God to work for you, do not exercise doubt in your mind. Doubt can also affect achievement. In his hometown, Christ did little for them because of their unbelief. See Matthew 13:53-58:

> "...And he did not do many miracles there because of their lack of faith."

DECEIT

Before going any further, it is worthy to note that "...*Satan himself masquerades as an angel of light.*" - 2 Corinthians 11:14.

Take the case of the man of God from Judah and the prophet of Bethel as an example. The latter deceived the former by lying.

Read 1 Kings 13:1-20. The question one would like to ask is: why didn't the man of God from Judah consult God to know if the instructions God gave him had changed? Remember that God spoke to him directly. The man of God from Judah died a horrible death as a result.

The devil also tried to deceive Jesus in the wilderness (Luke 4:1-13). As if the One who owns the earth needs any *'incentive'*, Satan offered Jesus authority and splendor in return for worship.

ANGER

The enemy uses this means to stop people from achieving their goals. Moses was angry over the people's complaint for water and subsequently struck the rock with the rod instead of speaking to the rock with the rod in his hand. Read Numbers 20:2-12.

David's anger against Nabal almost caused him to sin (1 Samuel 25:2-6). Read James 1:19-20.

LUST

Lust is a sexual craving that may lead to fornication or adultery. Read Proverbs 6:25 and 1 John 2:16. The example of David and Bathsheba in 2 Samuel 11:1-26 highlights what can happen when lust is not controlled. David had Bathsheba's husband, Uriah, killed. David did well before God except for this:

"...David had done what was right in the eyes of the Lord and had not failed to keep any of the Lord's commands all the days of his life-except in the case of Uriah the Hittite." - 1 King 15:5

GREED

It is human nature not to be satisfied, but the spirit of contentment should dwell in a Christian because "a greedy man brings trouble to his family" (Proverbs 15:27). This is true.

Look at 2 Kings 5:1-27 on how Gehazi extorted money from Naaman, whom God, through Elisha, healed of leprosy. Even though Naaman urged Elisha to receive gifts, he refused. But Gehazi thought his master was too easy on Naaman, so he sneaked away to demand gifts from him.

> "...My master sent me to say, 'Two young men from the company of the prophets have just come to me from the hill country of Ephraim. Please give them a talent of silver and two sets of clothing.'"
>
> - 2 Kings 5:22

Gehazi's action brought trouble not only on himself but on generations following him. Elisha pronounced that:

> "'Naaman's leprosy will cling to you and to your descendants forever.' Then Gehazi went from Elisha's presence and his skin was leprous - it had become as white as snow." - 2 Kings 5:26

Note this also:

> "...Watch out! Be on your guard against all kinds of greed; a man's life does not consist in the abundance of his possessions."
>
> - Luke 12:15.

PRIDE

This may be in the form of utterances or behaviour. The devil knows well that ... it is one of the seven things that are detestable to the Lord (Proverbs 6:16-19). Also,

> "Pride goes before destruction, a haughty spirit before a fall."
>
> - Proverbs 16:18

Study the case of Queen Vashti (Esther 1:1-12) and King Nebuchadnezzar (Daniel 4:29-32). When you do not thank God for the things you get from him, it is deemed as pride. What about the ungrateful Hezekiah? Find out in 2 Chronicles 32:24-26.

Deuteronomy 18 warns us not to forget the Lord. Do not say in your heart: "My power and the strength of my hands have produced this wealth for me."

DELAY

Sometimes, the answer or reply to our prayer may be delayed. There may be a reason for this; the forces that one cannot see may be an obstacle. Read Daniel 10:12-13. But the scripture tells us:

"Hope deferred makes the heart sick, but a longing fulfilled is a tree of life." - Proverbs 13:12

The devil deploys delay as a tactic to make the heart sick. Remember, Satan wants you to give up worshiping God, and he will try to frustrate you and negate promises such as:

"Ask and it will be given to you; seek and you will find; knock and the door will be opened to you. For everyone who asks receives; the one who seeks finds; and to the one who knocks, the door will be opened..." - Matthew 7:7-8

If the answer to your prayer is delayed, let the bible reference directly below comfort you. Abraham, Hannah, Zechariah, and Rachel each prayed for a child, but God answered each one of them in his own time with a child who had a purpose.

"And we know that in all things God works for the good of those who love Him, who have been called according to his purpose."

- Romans 8:28

HOW TO BE SPIRITUALLY ALERT

Apostle Paul viewed spiritual alertness from the preparedness of a fully armed Roman soldier. Look at Ephesians 6:11-17 KJV:

"[11] Put on the full armour of God, so that you can take your stand against the devil's schemes.

"¹² For our struggle is not against flesh and blood, but against the rulers, against the authorities, against the powers of this dark world, and against the spiritual forces of evil in the heavenly realms.

"¹³ Therefore put on the full armour of God, so that when the day of evil comes, you may be able to stand your ground, and after you have done everything, to stand.

"¹⁴ Stand firm then, with the belt of truth buckled around your waist, with the breastplate of righteousness in place,

"¹⁵ And with your feet fitted with the readiness that comes from the gospel of peace.

"¹⁶ In addition to all this, take up the shield of faith, with which you can extinguish all the flaming arrows of the evil one.

"¹⁷ Take the helmet of salvation and the sword of the Spirit, which is the word of God."

To illustrate what it means to put on the whole armour, take a look at the illustration of a fully armed Roman soldier below. You will notice that various parts of the body are protected by the helmet, body armour, shield, and sandals. The verses explain what each one of us should be doing. Really, 'words can paint a picture'.

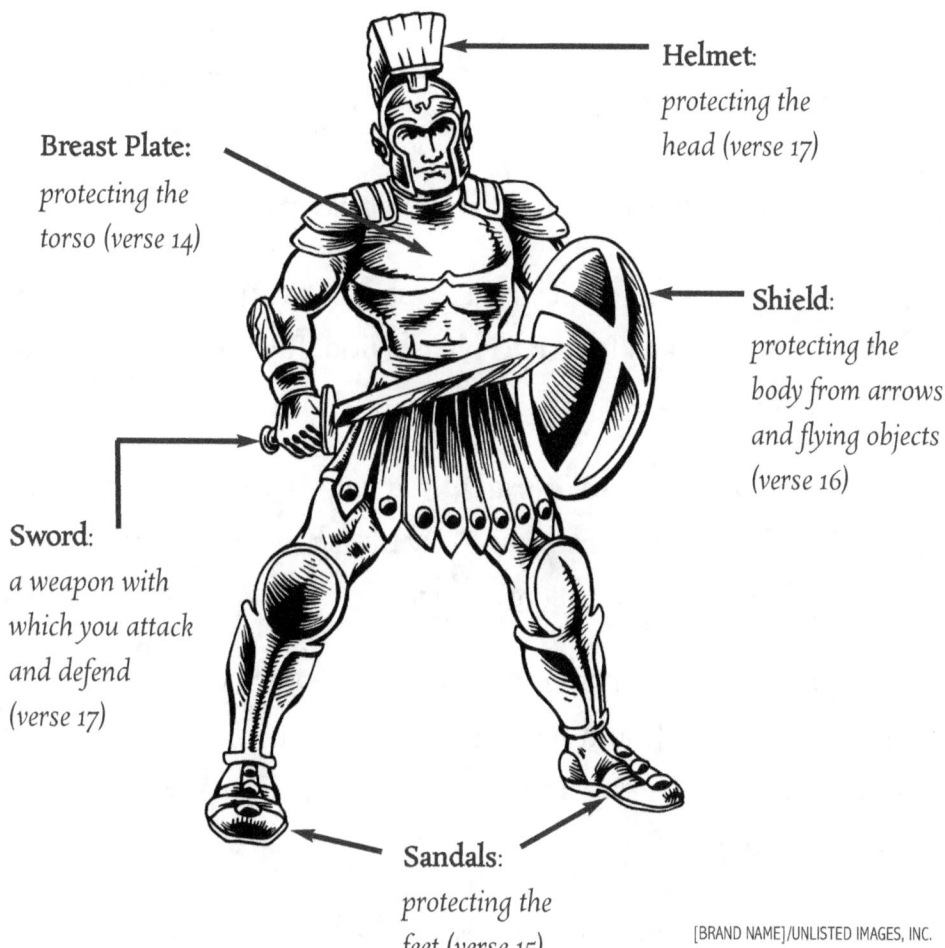

How to Please God

"Those controlled by the sinful nature cannot please God." - Romans 8:8

In dealing with this topic, let us look at how Apostle Paul urged the Thessalonians to live to please God. Read 1 Thessalonians 4:1-12. Let's look at verse 1:

> *"Finally, brothers, we instructed you how to live in order to please God, as in fact you are living. Now we ask you and urge you in the Lord Jesus to do this more and more."*

Living to please God is not what one should practice only in times of need; it should be continuous. That is, we should do it more and more (verses 1 and 10). Pleasing God involves more than the avoidance of sin.

THE THINGS WE OUGHT TO KNOW OR DO:

- It is essential to have faith in God for without faith it is impossible to please God (Hebrews 11:6).

- Worship the Lord with gladness (Psalm 100), dress modestly with decency and propriety (conformity to prevailing customs and usages), and in the time of prosperity we are to be joyful. Read 1 Timothy 2:8-9 and Deuteronomy 28:47 reads:

  > *"Because you did not serve the Lord your God joyfully and gladly in the time of prosperity, therefore in hunger and thirst..."*

- Offer your body as a living sacrifice.
    "Therefore, I urge you, brothers, in view of God's mercy, to offer your bodies as living sacrifices, holy and pleasing to God - this is your spiritual act of worship." - Romans 12:1

- Do good. Read Romans 2:9-10, Colossians 1:9-12, and Micah 6:6-8.
    "And do not forget to do good and to share with others, for with such sacrifices God is pleased." - Hebrews 13:16

- Work with all your heart.

    "Whatever you do, work at it with all your heart, as working for the Lord, not for men, since you know that you will receive an inheritance from the Lord as a reward. It is the Lord Christ you are serving." - Colossians 3:23-24

- Servants of God should not be men pleasers.
    Some men and women of God tend to please people so as to increase membership, but God gives genuine increase. Please read 1 Thessalonians 2:1-4. Now listen to this,

    "Am I now trying to win the approval of human beings, or of God? Or am I trying to please people? <u>If I were still trying to please people, I would not be a servant of Christ.</u>" - Galatians 1:10

Examples of people who pleased God:
- Jesus Christ pleased God. - Matthew 17:5, John 8:29, and 2 Peter 1:16-18
- By faith Enoch pleased God. - Hebrews 11:5
- Hannah also pleased God by fulfilling her vow. - 1 Samuel 2:18-21
- Abraham pleased God. - Hebrews 11:17

What happens when your ways please God?
Your enemies will be at peace with you. Proverbs 16:7 reads:

"When a man's ways are pleasing to the Lord, he makes even his enemies live at peace with him."

The Lord will bless you when you please God. Ecclesiastes 2:26:

"To the man who pleases him, God gives wisdom, knowledge, and happiness, but to the sinner he gives the task of gathering and storing up wealth to hand it over to the one who pleases God. This too is meaningless, a chasing after the wind."

Is Your Faith in Downturn?

In recent times, men's hearts have begun to fail for fear of the economic downturn. Even many nations, including the super powers, are either perplexed or puzzled. Solutions are sought from the same people who brought us the *"Chip & Pin."* Is any nation turning to God yet? In Genesis 41:54-56, there was also a global meltdown when a famine was over all the face of the earth. During this period, there was no Chip and neither was there Pin, but there was Joseph. Egypt turned to a man who operated with the Spirit of God. Pharaoh described him as discreet and wise. Concerning wealth management, let us look at what the scripture says:

> *"Be sure you know the condition of your flocks, give careful attention to your herds."* - Proverbs 27:23

Take a look at this report:

> "The issue of a rise in suicide rates during times of recession isn't limited to the UK of course, and in the USA, Good Morning America reporter Chris Cuomo explained that the personal finances of some U.S. citizens "have people so stressed, they are developing health problems."

His report continued and he stated,

> "The link between financial troubles and psychological problems is well documented." He added, "In the U.S. the seminal example is the Great Depression, when the suicide rate jumped from 14 to 17 for every 100,000 Americans."

He concluded with this thought: "And today, with the threat of recession looming large, the price we pay physically may skyrocket as well."

I say with confidence in the Lord that we will pay no such price. Amen. Didn't the bible say, *"A heart at peace gives life to the body..."* (Proverbs 14:30)? And if the hearts of men are failing, it is because of unbelief and the lack of knowledge of the scriptures.

There were great famines in the days of old. During that of Samaria (2 King 5:25-33, 7:1-20), one man did not believe that the Hand of God could alleviate people's hardship. He saw it happen but did not eat thereof. Again, this was due to unbelief. Now, if this man perished because of his unbelief, would he have believed that a Messiah would be conceived by the Holy Spirit and that the same would die and be raised from the dead on the third day? Can this man's soul be saved? This is a subject for the bible class. If you do not believe in the prophets of God (that we see), it is probable that you won't believe in God.

> "Believe in the Lord your God, so shall ye be established; believe his prophets, so shall ye prosper." - 2 Chronicles 20:20

If in doubt, take a look at this:

> "You may say to yourselves, "How can we know when a message has not been spoken by the Lord?" If what a prophet proclaims in the name of the Lord does not take place or come true, that is a message the Lord has not spoken. That prophet has spoken presumptuously, so do not be alarmed." - Deuteronomy 18:21-22

There were also people who doubted the resurrection of Christ in the generation that witnessed his birth, the miracles He performed, and his death on the cross, all of which were foretold. Our generation read about it, it is preached to us on the pulpit and across several forms of electronic media, and it is no surprise that many people (in this generation) do not believe that he rose from the dead, let alone that Christ will return. That Christ will return can be proved using a simple logic: If the prophecies concerning Christ are true (they came to pass), then the prophecies Christ gave are also true (will come to pass).

Question: Is there any prophecy in the bible concerning Christ that is yet to be fulfilled?
If you answered 'No', read Luke 21, the Lord will give the understanding. Now, if you answered 'Yes', is it about *"The Son of man coming in a cloud with power and great glory"*? Do you believe

this? If you do, are you prepared? Either of these two things will happen to all: Christ may come before your death, or your death may precede the coming of Christ.

This brings to mind the 2009 Malaysian Formula One Grand Prix. Heavy rain halted the race after 32 of the 56 scheduled laps, and the man in front, Jenson Button, not Toyota's Jarno Trulli, was declared the winner.

Life is also a race. Unlike Formula One, there will be many winners through the grace of God (for by grace we are saved through faith), and the prize is not perishable. But like Formula One, some races will be cut short. That is, people may not live up to the expected age. Don't get caught in the *Pit Lane* or delay in *exerting effort or energy to win*. You began the race when you were born; the race ends when you die or at the coming of Christ.

Brethren, every race has an end and so does every famine, but your faith must know no downturn. In no small measure, I give glory to God for restoring my penmanship without my own hook.

Will the Almighty Pervert Justice?

When a person is convicted and punished for a crime that he or she did not commit, primarily it is called Miscarriage of Justice. There is also Wrongful Conviction, a conviction reached in an unfair or disputed trial. This is synonymous with Miscarriage of Justice. Human beings may err in justice, but the judgement of God is pure.

> "What then shall we say? Is God unjust? Not at all!"
> - Romans 9:14

Assuming that the 'An eye for an eye, and a tooth for a tooth' law is in place, what would be the likely sin committed for each of the following punishments?
1. A man's business was ruined on the same day all his employees were killed but one.
2. A serious illness struck a man so that he could barely lie down on his back or sit down.
3. The roof of a house collapsed, killing a man's sons and daughters.

Any of the three calamities listed above is enough to devastate a man with strong resolve. But a blameless man, Job, who shunned evil, was afflicted by all in just one day. Let us assume Job lived in the same time as Moses and with the 'An eye for an eye, and a tooth for a tooth' law in place. Job may have committed the following offenses:

1. Falsely acquired a neighbour business and killed all the employees but one.
2. Used voodoo to cause a man to suffer unbearable illness.
3. Killed someone else's children.

But Job was blameless. Like him, you may have suffered afflictions where you cannot possibly recall a sin you may have committed to justify what you are going through or may have gone through. You may think it is not justified, but can you appoint a day in court with God? Who will mediate for you?

> "For he is not a man, as I am, that I might answer Him, that we should come to trial together. There is no umpire between us, who might lay his hand upon us both." - Job 9:32-33

Can you imagine that a Nebraska Democratic State Senator, Ernie Chambers, decided to go straight to the court in an effort to stop natural disasters from befalling the world? Imagine this: Chambers bases his ability to sue God as "that defendant, being omnipresent [f], is personally present in Douglas County." A year later on the 16th of October 2008, the case was thrown out because God has an unlisted address. Where would you serve God a notice or court summons?

WILL THE ALMIGHTY PERVERT JUSTICE? | 297

Story link: http://www.foxnews.com/story/0,2933,297121,00.html

A Romanian prisoner also sued God for failing to save him from the devil. This time, God's offenses were: *"cheating, abuse, and traffic of influence."*

Listen to this: "He added: 'God even claimed and received from me various goods and prayers in exchange for forgiveness and the promise that I would be rid of problems and have a better life.'" But prosecutors in this case said it would probably be dropped because they were unable to subpoena God to court. *Story link: http://www.ananova.com/news/story/sm_1576068.html*

Like Job, you may even assert your innocence (Job 31), but who will plead for you? Job said:

> *"...I am innocent, but God denies me justice."* - Job 34:5

Like Job, you may have been mocked, friends may utterly detest you and even keep far from you, your prosperity may have passed like a cloud, and you may have cried out to God without answers (Job 30). And yet, you cannot contend with Him.

> *"If one wished to contend with him, one could not answer him once in a thousand times. He is wise in heart, and mighty in strength–who has hardened himself against Him, and succeeded?"*
>
> *- Job 9:3-4*

It is good to know that our righteousness has nothing to offer God, and our wickedness does not affect him. Our goodness is to a man like us, and when we do evil, it affects a fellow being, not God (Job 35:6-8). Job had integrity but God is supreme.

What did Job do after all of these events? He repented, saying:

> "I have uttered what I did not understand, things too wonderful for me, which I did not know ... therefore I despise myself, and repent in dust and ashes." - Job 42:1-6

Not only were Job's fortunes restored, but God also gave him longevity so that he enjoyed these restored fortunes. To see two generations is a blessing; to see four generations is more than a double boon. Job did not have to write a will; he was alive to distribute inheritance to his sons and daughters (Job 42:12-16). A similar grace can still be enjoyed today. If it happened before, we can still be benefactors of the same type of grace today.

If you have been afflicted like Job and you have contended with God, repent. And like Job, your fortunes will be restored by Jehovah, and your latter days will be blessed more than your beginning. Amen.

If you are afflicted or persecuted far beyond your ability to endure, you are not alone. Don't give up. Look at this from Paul the Apostle:

> "He has delivered us from such a deadly peril, and he will deliver us again. On him we have set our hope that he will continue to deliver us, as you help us by your prayers." - 2 Corinthians 1:10

You may not like this but to keep us from having a high opinion of ourselves or our accomplishments, God sometimes allows or does what we do not expect. To understand this, consider that *"God did extraordinary miracles through Paul"* (Acts 19:11), but he refused to take away that thorn in his flesh.

> "...Therefore, in order to keep me from becoming conceited, I was given a thorn in my flesh, a messenger of Satan, to torment me. [8] Three times I pleaded with the Lord to take it away from me. [9] But he said to me, "My grace is sufficient for you, for my power is made perfect in weakness." Therefore I will boast all the more gladly about my weaknesses, so that Christ's power may rest on me."
> - 2 Corinthians 12:7-9

Let me conclude with the words of the preacher:

> "When times are good, be happy; but when times are bad, consider this: God has made the one as well as the other. Therefore, no one can discover anything about their future." - Ecclesiastes 7:14

---

f) **Omnipresent** means present in all places at the same time.

God's Team Working

Companies or institutions wishing to stay ahead of the competition usually provide their employees with training, and they encourage and promote teamwork. Training provided may include leadership skills, understanding the criteria for success, and managing resources. Challenges may also form part of the curriculum. All of these efforts are initiated because companies want to succeed. Today, a church would need to do the same to succeed in fishing men and preparing them for the Kingdom of Heaven.

Surprisingly, God, who has the ability to do all, does not do it alone. At creation, God said:

> "...Let us make man in our image, after our likeness: and let them have dominion over the fish of the sea, and over the fowl of the air, and over the cattle, and over all the earth, and over every creeping thing that creepeth upon the earth." - Genesis 1:26

So man was created with the qualities that are comparable to those in the team that created him. That is not all; he (man) was given authority over what God had earlier created.

Knowing the ability of what he created, the Almighty approached man to name all other creatures:

> "So out of the ground the Lord God formed every beast of the field and every bird of the air and brought them to the man to see what he would call them; and whatever the man called every living creature, that was its name." - Genesis 2:19

The helper made for him he also named:

> "...and the rib which the Lord God had taken from the man he made into a woman and brought her to the man. Then the man said, 'This at last is bone of my bones and flesh of my flesh; she shall be called Woman, because she was taken out of Man.'"
> - Genesis 2:22-23

Notice that God approached the man he created twice to name the creatures. This is not because he could not do it; it was God's way of team working. In God, there is no arrogance or overbearing pride despite his superiority. To man he gives challenges as would good bosses to their employees.

In some special cases, God gave names to people before conception or birth. John the Baptist, who was sent to make straight the path for Jesus, was named before his mother conceived him. The man described in Isaiah 9:6-8 needs no other man to smooth his path because he can do everything; he is the Mighty God.

There is no doubt that man was created to be inventive. A group set out to make a name for itself by building a tower with its top in the heavens. To stop this from happening, God called his team to work.

> *"Come, let us go down, and there confuse their language, that they may not understand one another's speech."* - Genesis 11:7

Instead of building a tower again, men built a space shuttle and sent it to the moon in 1969. They also unveiled a plaque bearing President Nixon's signature and an inscription reading:

> *"Here men from the planet Earth first set foot upon the Moon July 1969 AD. We came in peace for all mankind."*

Unlike Babel, the exploration to the moon was for peace and not in disagreement with God's instruction. To date, man in flesh cannot explore heaven, but he was given the grace to explore the moon after several manned and unmanned Apollo missions.

As a little boy, I often wondered why God doesn't write in the sky for us to read. Instead he wrote twice on stones. To tell us his set of rules, he wrote on stone tablets. The Holy One who made rain, snow, and sleet could have made leaflets and air-dropped them in the areas inhabited by man. Instead he sent Moses.

In John 1:17 the division of labor is clearly shown: *"For the law was given through Moses; grace and truth came through Jesus Christ."* Moses too did not work alone; God chose Aaron to speak for him because he was not eloquent in speech. Here, God leaves man to wonder why he did not cure Moses' speech defect, a man through whom he wrought many miracles. Neither did Christ work alone; he chose twelve disciples to work with him and taught them. His disciples also asked questions. That is, one who is taught must also be wise.

After Moses, God sent prophets from Isaiah to Malachi. After all of them, Christ came; and after Christ many founders, general overseers, reverends, bishops, and pastors. The question is, are all like Christ? He was in the form of God but was made of no reputation as a servant in the form of a man. See Philippians 2:5-8.

Christ gave spiritual gifts to men for the edification of the body of Christ (the church).

> *"And his gifts were that some should be apostles, some prophets, some evangelists, some pastors and teachers, to equip the saints for the work of ministry, for building up the body of Christ, until we all attain to the unity of the faith and of the knowledge of the Son of God, to mature manhood..."* - Ephesians 4:11-15

Any church wishing to succeed in its mission must pray that members receive and use these gifts for the purpose of edifying the church. Rarely can a single vessel possess all the gifts. If that is the case, there will be no division of labour or teamwork.

When a seed is dropped on a rock, it rarely grows, but when it lands on a fertile ground where it can flourish, it will grow. And if nurtured, it will bring forth fruits, and fruits well preserved will see the harvest. The same goes for the church. Christ told Peter three times: *"feed my flock."*

Try listening to or watching these two perform: a one-man band and an orchestra. Although they both play music, the difference is clear. In a one-man band, an individual does all while an orchestra has several instrument groups and is directed by a conductor. A symphony (by an orchestra) can range from forty minutes to over an hour while a live performance by a one-man band lasting five minutes without gasping for breath should be classed as a stunt. A church whose major duties are performed by an individual is like a one-man band. Usually, it doesn't grow and seldom lasts.

Seventy Elders Chosen to Assist Moses
To share the burden of the people with Moses, the Lord told him:

"...Bring me seventy of Israel's elders who are known to you as

leaders and officials among the people. Have them come to the tent of meeting, that they may stand there with you. ¹⁷ *I will come down and speak with you there, and I will take some of the power of the Spirit that is on you and put it on them. They will share the burden of the people with you so that you will not have to carry it alone."*

- Numbers 11:16-17

Just as Moses did, leaders should make an effort in presenting their cases before God. If your congregation is wailing at you, ask for more people (who are God-fearing) to bear the burden with you.

Is Your Pastor or Shepherd a Joshua?

At a time when men and women are going here and there in search of knowledge, it is essential that you worship under good leadership at least. We were warned: perilous times are here. If you are looking for a sanctuary, look for one where its leadership is characterized by the qualities seen in Joshua.

JOSHUA WAS INAUGURATED

A leadership that did not commence formally or officially is likely to show overbearing pride. Why? He or she was not inaugurated by a superior.

Joshua was Moses' assistant since youth (Numbers 11:28), and the man who knew God face to face (Moses) was instructed to inaugurate Joshua to lead Israel (Numbers 27:18-20 and Deuteronomy 31:23).

What is the importance of inauguration?

Apart from bestowing authority on the person inaugurated, the Spirit of Wisdom is also given. Note this:

> *"Now Joshua son of Nun was filled with the spirit of wisdom because Moses had laid his hands on him. So the Israelites listened to him and did what the Lord had commanded Moses."*
>
> - Deuteronomy 34:9

Wisdom comes with other qualities: humility (Proverbs 11:2), prudence, knowledge, and discretion (Proverbs 8:12). It is good to know that having the Spirit of Wisdom surpasses formal education. The latter is not required for good leadership. Joshua had no formal education.

THE FEAR OF GOD

This quality is essential for the success of any leader. Joshua's willingness to do according to what God instructed showed he had the fear of God. He carefully obeyed God's instructions on what to do concerning Jericho. He marched round the city of Jericho once for six days and seven times on the seventh day as instructed. Joshua did not assume 'grace' as some would by marching round the city only once on the seventh day (Joshua 6:2-20).

He crossed River Jordan 'at flood stage' when the risk of drowning was highest, following the instruction of God (Joshua 3:14-17). When faced with armies with as many people as the sand on the seashore, Joshua was not afraid. He hamstrung their horses and burned their chariots with fire (Joshua 11:6-9, as instructed by God.

He had all men circumcised again (Joshua 5:2), as instructed. In all, he carefully obeyed the voice of God ... And it was well with him. Joshua was never a men-pleaser.

WISDOM

Joshua's overall planning and conduct was very effective. He sent two spies to Jericho; he did not just go for it. He consulted with God when faced with failure or difficulties. He was decisive in the case of the Gibeonites, who pretended they were from the far country when they were really neighbours.

COURAGE

God and Moses continually told Joshua to be courageous. This quality was essential to deal with fear and carry along a people filled with unbelief. Can a Christian accomplish great things without courage? Read Deuteronomy 20:3-4.

HAVE YOU SEEN THE FOLLOWING MANIFESTING?

Looking at Isaiah 61:1-7. When you worship under an anointed man of God, the works of the Holy Spirit will be easily noticed.

1. Preaching of the good news (with emphasis on the return of Christ) - Malachi 2:7 points out:

   "For the lips of a priest ought to preserve knowledge, because he is the messenger of the Lord Almighty and people seek instruction from his mouth."

2. Broken hearts mending
3. Captives being set free
4. Gladness instead of mourning
5. Ashes turning to beauty
6. Reproach turning to glory
7. Prosperity

The entire congregation may not be faithful to the Lord, like Joshua, but an anointed leader will carry along the majority by constantly reminding them of God's deeds. Look at Joshua 24:1-14.

> "Israel served the Lord throughout the lifetime of Joshua and of the elders who outlived him and who had experienced everything the Lord had done for Israel." - Joshua 24:31

EXCEPTIONAL CASES

There may be exceptional cases like that of Paul and Moses. There are two points here:

Moses had once killed, and Paul persecuted the church of God in his early days. The anointed man of God under whom you worship may have done similar things in his early days. It does not mean the anointed man of God under whom you worship is not called. A testament to this is the statement below:

> "I was personally unknown to the churches of Judea that are in Christ. They only heard the report: 'The man who formerly persecuted us is now preaching the faith he once tried to destroy.' And they praised God because of me." - Galatians 1:22-24

Saul named Paul did not consult anyone. Only Ananias prayed for him to regain his sight. - Acts 9:10-18

> *"...I did not consult any man, nor did I go up to Jerusalem to see those who were apostles before I was."* - Galatians 1:15-17

Likewise, God called Moses while no one was present. The account of the might of God in the lives of these two men is there for all to read in the bible.

CAUTION!

There is a common mistake in churches today. Should anyone who wants to become a priest be consecrated? It has happened in the past and it is happening today. Should we not advise caution in choosing pastors and shepherds?

> *"Even after this, Jeroboam did not change his evil ways, but once more appointed priests for the high places from all sorts of people.* **Anyone who wanted to become a priest he consecrated for the high places.** *This was the sin of the house of Jeroboam that led to its downfall and to its destruction from the face of the earth."*
>
> - 1 Kings 13:33-34

Judgement may not rest with man, but God does not show favouritism (Romans 2:11).

YOUR SPIRITUAL RESPONSIBILITY TO YOUR PASTOR

If pastors and shepherds bear the burden of the congregation, it is the spiritual responsibility of the members to pray for them. Although they have the authority of God vested in them, they still need prayers. The bible pointed out in James 5:17 that "Elijah was a human being, even as we are." That is, men and women of God can be corrupted or tempted. It is a sin if your pastor or shepherd does not pray for you. If in doubt, please read 1 Samuel 12:23.

When Apostles Barnabas and Paul were treated like gods in Lystra (Acts 14:8-18), they promptly corrected their worshippers, saying, *"Friends, why are you doing this? We too are only human, like you."* Men and women of God are to be revered but not equated to God.

Therefore, if we profess that we care for our leaders, prayers ought to be made for them so that they may lead a godly life that is pleasing to God.

WHY IT IS NECESSARY TO PRAY FOR YOUR PASTOR.

Look at the two examples below on how leaders can make mistakes:

- David's unauthorized census caused the death of 70,000 people from Dan to Beersheba (2 Samuel 24:1-16).

- King Hezekiah exposed his wealth to the Babylonian envoys to the detriment of his own people. He was showing off.

  "Hezekiah received the envoys and showed them all that was in his storehouses - the silver, the gold, the spices, and the fine olive oil - his armory and everything found among his treasures. There was nothing in his palace or in all his kingdom that Hezekiah did not show them." - 2 Kings 20:13

After this, the Lord sent the prophet Isaiah to tell him:

"The time will surely come when everything in your palace, and all that your predecessors have stored up until this day, will be carried off to Babylon. Nothing will be left, says the Lord. And some of your descendants, your own flesh and blood who will be born to you, will be taken away, and they will become eunuchs in the palace of the king of Babylon." - 2 Kings 20:17-18

Instead of entreating the Lord for mercy on behalf of his people, Hezekiah shrugged off the message. Listen to his reply:

"'The word of the Lord you have spoken is good,' Hezekiah replied. For he thought, 'Will there not be peace and security in my lifetime?'"
- 2 Kings 20:19

Isaiah's prophecy above came to pass. Read Jeremiah 52:12-30.

But what does the scripture say about praying for our elders or the leadership? Look at 1 Timothy 2:1-3:

> "I urge, then, first of all, that petitions, prayers, intercession, and thanksgiving be made for all people - for kings and all those in authority, that we may live peaceful and quiet lives in all godliness and holiness. This is good, and pleases God our Savior, who wants all people to be saved and to come to a knowledge of the truth."

There are two things here:
1. It is good and acceptable in the sight of God to pray for our leaders...
2. ...that we may live peaceful and quiet lives in all godliness and holiness.

Apostle Paul requested we do it (pray for church leaders).

> "As for other matters, brothers and sisters, **pray for us** that the message of the Lord may spread rapidly and be honoured, just as it was with you. And pray that we may be delivered from wicked and evil people, for not everyone has faith." - 2 Thessalonians 3:1-2

> "Devote yourselves to prayer, being watchful and thankful. **And pray for us**, too, that God may open a door for our message, so that we may proclaim the mystery of Christ, for which I am in chains."
> - Colossians 4:2-3

Prayer in relation to shepherds and flock is a two-way thing. They pray for you; you pray for them. Now, pray for your pastor.

Jesus Knows You by Name

If you are a manufacturer, you will name your products. For example, there is Diet Pepsi and Pepsi Max. Both are similar products made by the same manufacturer. Since God created mankind, everyone has a name, but he seldom gets into the business of naming people. He has left that for us to do. Logically, if God knows your name and Jesus said, "...the Father is in me, and I in the Father" (John 10:38), then Jesus knows you by name.

There are several instances in the bible where God and Jesus called individuals by name. To bring the Israelites out of Egypt, God called out to Moses.

> "When the Lord saw that he had gone over to look, God called to him from within the bush, '**Moses! Moses!**' And Moses said, 'Here I am.'" - Exodus 3:4

Pharaoh's daughter gave Moses his name, but God continually assured Moses by saying, "I know you by name." Read Exodus 33:12,17. God assured Israel in the same manner in Isaiah 45:1-3.

To inform that "The guilt of Eli's house will never be atoned for by sacrifice or offering," God called Samuel to relay the message.

> "Then the Lord called **Samuel**. ...A third time the Lord called, 'Samuel!'..." - 1 Samuel 3:4-8

For Abram and his wife, Sarai, there was a change of name.

> "Abram fell facedown, and God said to him, 'As for me, this is my covenant with you: You will be the father of many nations. No longer will you be called **Abram**; your name will be Abraham, for I have made you a father of many nations.' ... God also said to Abraham, 'As for **Sarai** your wife, you are no longer to call her Sarai; her name will be Sarah.'" - Genesis 17:3-5

To identify a skillful man for building works, God spoke to Moses:

> "Then the LORD said to Moses, 'See, I have chosen **Bezalel son of Uri**, the son of Hur, of the tribe of Judah...'" - Exodus 31:2

To avoid confusion, God named the man to succeed Moses and the priest to conduct the swearing in.

> "So the Lord said to Moses, 'Take **Joshua son of Nun**, a man in whom is the spirit of leadership, and lay your hand on him. Have him stand before **Eleazar the priest** and the entire assembly and

commission him in their presence. Give him some of your authority so the whole Israelite community will obey him.'"

- Numbers 27:18-20

But the task of anointing a king to succeed Saul was not made easy for Samuel. Apart from being risky, since Saul was still on the throne, he was given only the family name of the successor and he had to choose from eight men.

> "...'I am sending you to **Jesse of Bethlehem**. I have chosen one of his sons to be king.' But Samuel said, 'How can I go? If Saul hears about it, he will kill me.'" - 1 Samuel 16:1-2

While passing through Jericho, Jesus stayed the night with a man he called by name. Jesus saw his effort and the desire to see him.

> "Jesus entered Jericho and was passing through. A man was there by the name of Zacchaeus; he was a chief tax collector and was wealthy. He wanted to see who Jesus was, but because he was short, he could not see over the crowd. So he ran ahead and climbed a sycamore-fig tree to see Him, since Jesus was coming that way. When Jesus reached the spot, he looked up and said to him, '**Zacchaeus**, come down immediately. I must stay at your house today.' So he came down at once and welcomed Him gladly."

- Luke 19:1-6

Most pertinent to this topic is John 1:42-48:

> "And he brought him to Jesus. Jesus looked at him and said, 'You are **Simon son of John**. You will be called Cephas' (which, when translated, is Peter). The next day Jesus decided to leave for Galilee. Finding Philip, he said to him, 'Follow me.' **Philip**, like Andrew and Peter, was from the town of Bethsaida. Philip found Nathanael and told him, 'We have found the one Moses wrote about in the Law, and about whom the prophets also wrote - Jesus of Nazareth, the son of Joseph.' ... When Jesus saw Nathanael approaching, he said of him, '**Here truly is an Israelite in whom there is no deceit.**'... 'How do you know me?' Nathanael asked. Jesus answered, 'I saw you while you were still under the fig tree before Philip called you.'"

Not only does Christ know your name, but he knows your heart, what you are doing, and your place of birth. He described Nathanael as an Israelite in whom there is no deceit. The one who determines the number of the stars and calls them each by name (Psalm 147:3-5) knows everything about you, for the Lord searches every heart and understands every desire and every thought (1 Chronicles 28:9). If the Lord knows your heart, he knows your afflictions and heart desires.

When there was no water for Ishmael to drink in the wilderness of Beersheba, the Lord called unto his mother, Hagar, and showed her a well of water.

"God heard the boy crying, and the angel of God called to Hagar from heaven and said to her, 'What is the matter, **Hagar**? Do not be afraid; God has heard the boy crying as he lies there. Lift the boy up and take him by the hand, for I will make him into a great nation.' Then God opened her eyes and she saw a well of water. So she went and filled the skin with water and gave the boy a drink."

- Genesis 21:17-19

The Lord will not forget your needs. The same God that gave Ishmael water when he was thirsting to death commanded the ravens to feed Elijah twice a day by the brook of Kerith.

"Then the word of the Lord came to Elijah: 'Leave here, turn eastward, and hide in the **Kerith Ravine**, east of the Jordan. You will drink from the brook, and I have directed the ravens to supply you with food there.' So he did what the LORD had told him. He went to the Kerith Ravine, east of the Jordan, and stayed there. The ravens brought him bread and meat in the morning and bread and meat in the evening, and he drank from the brook." - 1 Kings 17:2-6

There are other instances where God sent angels to named persons. For example, the birth of John the Baptist was foretold by an angel. The prophecy told to Zechariah by this angel named him, his wife, and the child so desired by the couple.

"...Do not be afraid, **Zechariah**; your prayer has been heard. Your

*wife **Elizabeth** will bear you a son, and you are to call him **John**..."*
- Luke 1:11-17

Today, similar grace is enjoyed by some Christians the world over. I benefited from such grace six years before my first daughter, Maria, was born. The name, Maria, was given in a prophecy by a ten-year-old boy.

Whatever your needs, whatever your afflictions, and however little you think you are, he alone knows. Because he knows, always call on him who knows you by name. He can give you more than you need, including salvation.

Army without Weapons

When you consider that God made the people who constitute an army, then it should not be difficult to understand that the Maker can destroy what he made using whatever means are at his disposal. And if the Lord is a man of war (Exodus 15:3), he definitely has some potent weapons and ammunitions in his arsenal. He has weapons with which to attack the faculties of hearing, sight, and equilibrium. But when fighting a war, men are constantly trying to outwit each other by using various military tactics.

As the Philistines pitched to fight against Israel during the era of King Saul, they tried what can be equated to a war of attrition.

> "Not a blacksmith could be found in the whole land of Israel, because the Philistines had said, 'Otherwise the Hebrews will make swords or spears!'
> [20]So all Israel went down to the Philistines to have their ploughshares, mattocks, axes and sickles sharpened."
> - 1 Samuel 13:19-20

The Philistines used a simple tactic to reduce the effectiveness of Saul's army such that 'on the day of the battle not a soldier with Saul and Jonathan had a sword or spear in his hand; only Saul and his son Jonathan had them.' But how would Israel fight without weapons? When you have the Lord who is a man of war behind you, he will outsmart your enemy. The Lord acted on the soldiers' behalf as Jonathan prayed.

> "Jonathan said to his young armour-bearer, 'Come, let's go over to the outpost of those uncircumcised fellows. Perhaps the Lord will act on our behalf. Nothing can hinder the Lord from saving, whether by many or by few.'" - 1 Samuel 14:6

To aid Saul and Jonathan, God caused a panic in the enemy's camp; **the ground shook.** And when "Saul and all his men assembled and went to the battle. They found the Philistines in total confusion, striking each other with their swords." - 1 Samuel 14:20

Before the era of Saul, when Samuel led Israel, the rulers of the Philistines came up to attack Israel at Mizpah. This time, "...**the Lord thundered with loud thunder** against the Philistines and threw them into such a panic that they were routed before the Israelites" (1 Samuel 7:10). And when you have a God who thunders so loudly, your enemies will be at peace with you.

> "So the Philistines were subdued and did not invade Israelite territory again. Throughout Samuel's lifetime, the hand of the Lord was against the Philistines" - 1 Samuel 7:13

Apart from earthquake and thunder, there are other weapons in God's arsenal. When God decided to give relief to the people of Samaria who experienced a famine when they were besieged by the entire army of the king of Aram, he used another method to disquiet the enemy.

> "...the Lord had caused the Arameans to hear **the sound of chariots and horses and a great army**, so that they said to one another, 'Look, the king of Israel has hired the Hittite and Egyptian kings to attack us!'" - 2 Kings 7:6

Without taking anything, the Arameans left their camp and ran for their lives. When you consider that an entire army camped against Samaria and left the camp as it was without taking anything, what the Israelites got from plundering the Arameans' camp would be a lot of supplies meant for the entire army. Rightly so, for:

> "...the people went out and plundered the camp of the Arameans. So a seah of flour sold for a shekel, and two seahs of barley sold for a shekel, as the Lord had said." - 2 Kings 7:16

Please read 2 Kings 7:1-2.

Having confidence in the Lord can make a world of difference when fighting a just war. When a vast army comprising the

Moabites and Ammonites, along with some of the Meunites, came against Jehoshaphat, after fasting and prayer, the Lord assured Jehoshaphat and the whole of Judah through his prophet, saying,

> *"Do not be afraid or discouraged because of this vast army. For the battle is not yours, but God's."* - 2 Chronicles 20:15

Jehoshaphat became confident and he told his people,

> *"Have faith in the Lord your God and you will be upheld; have faith in his prophets and you will be successful."* - 2 Chronicles 20:20

When you are oozing with confidence, you sometimes do the unusual. Jehoshaphat's battle array was different; he appointed singers to walk ahead of the army and the singers praised the Lord for his holy splendour. Now that they had left everything for God, this time, he (God) used a military tactic and confusion against the enemies. Jehoshaphat and his army did not use their weapons as the military alliance between the Moabites and Ammonites and some of the Meunites turned into confusion. Amazing! I wonder if there were army uniforms in those days.

> *"As they began to sing and praise,* **the Lord set ambushes** *against the men of Ammon and Moab and Mount Seir who were invading Judah, and they were defeated.* 23 *The men of Ammon and Moab*

> *rose up against the men from Mount Seir to destroy and annihilate them. After they finished slaughtering the men from Seir, they helped to destroy one another.* ²⁴ *When the men of Judah came to the place that overlooks the desert and looked towards the vast army, they saw only dead bodies lying on the ground; no-one had escaped."*
>
> - 2 Chronicles 20:22-24

What would you do if five nations rose against you? Consider the ratio (5 to 1) and bring back to mind God's promise: *Five of you will chase a hundred'*. Read Leviticus 26:7-8. When five kings with their troops moved against Gibeon and attacked it, Joshua and his entire army came to their rescue. As if confusion as a weapon was not adequate, **"the Lord hurled large hailstones** down on them from the sky, and more of them died from the hailstones than were killed by the swords of the Israelites." Read Joshua 10:1-11.

When Sennacherib, the King of Assyria, threatened King Hezekiah and all the people in the city of Jerusalem to silence the blasphemous king, God sent just one angel to destroy completely all the fighting men, the leaders, and the officers in the camp of the Assyrian king (2 Chronicles 32:9-23).

> *"And **the Lord sent an angel**, who annihilated all the fighting men and the leaders and officers in the camp of the Assyrian king. So he withdrew to his own land in disgrace. And when he went into*

the temple of his god, some of his sons cut him down with the sword. ²² So the Lord saved Hezekiah and the people of Jerusalem from the hand of Sennacherib king of Assyria and from the hand of all others. He took care of them on every side."

- 2 Chronicles 32:21-22

Men of God can also use weapons from God's arsenal. Before the Arameans besieged Samaria, Elisha and his servant went out one morning and saw that an army with horses and chariots had surrounded the city. What followed was amazing.

"As the enemy came down towards him, Elisha prayed to the Lord, **'Strike these people with blindness.'** *So he struck them with blindness, as Elisha had asked. ¹⁹ Elisha told them, 'This is not the road and this is not the city. Follow me, and I will lead you to the man you are looking for.' And he led them to Samaria."*

- 2 Kings 6:18-19

Apart from the blindness used in entrapping the Arameans, there were horses and chariots of fire all round Elisha that the naked eyes could not see. Please read 2 Kings 6:8-20.

Today, weapons of war have changed considerably and an army can mount attack on enemies from land, air, and sea using smart bombs. But God and his mighty weapons have not changed. When you are not fighting against flesh-and-blood enemies, you will still need God's mighty weapons. Remember that one of the benefits of serving the Lord is that no weapon turned against you will succeed (Isaiah 54:17). Also consider that if the word of God is living and active and it is sharper than any double-edged sword (Hebrews 4:12), then God is much more powerful. If your enemies think they are smart, the Lord will outsmart them only if you put your trust in him. Remember this when you pray:

> "Devise your strategy, but it will be thwarted; propose your plan, but it will not stand, for God is with us." - Isaiah 8:10

Be encouraged for "Jesus Christ is the same yesterday, today, and forever."

Spiritual Gym

*"For **physical training is of some value**, but godliness has value for all things, holding promise for both the present life and the life to come."*
- 1 Timothy 4:8

Appropriate levels of bodily activities are important for good health since they can enhance physical fitness and overall wellness. In fact, health experts concur that 'it's important that physical activity is a part of life for children, adults, and older people.' Exercise has some benefits: It can help you maintain a healthy weight and it can delay or prevent diabetes, some cancers, and heart problems.

Nearly every television channel runs an advert or documentary on health and fitness, and you will find the same in newspapers and magazines; the internet also carries these advertisements. The desire to look good and keep fit draws people to fitness classes at least once or twice a week and they spend an average of thirty minutes a day on physical activities. If you regularly exercise or spend time in the gym, you have done no wrong. **But what have you done to exercise the spirit?** Exercising the spirit includes praying, fasting, singing hymns, reading and discussing the scriptures, and attending revival services and normal church services.

Did you know? *"Food for the stomach and the stomach for food - but God will destroy them both..."* - 1 Corinthians 6:13

Quite a number of people desire a perfect physical body and they will go to great lengths to tone muscles, attain a six-pack stomach, and enhance all the noticeable body features. Those who already have these sought-after fitness results will agree they cannot be achieved within a short time. Acquiring them is a gradual process that requires a strict diet plan and exercise regimen.

Guess what? The toned body you so desire will one day be destroyed and will rise again for judgement another day. Remember, the things of the world will perish with the world. Therefore, look beyond good looks because there is also a spiritual body that needs toning. Listen to this:

> *"...If there is a natural body, there is also a spiritual body."*
> - 1 Corinthians 15:44

There are verses in the bible pointing to the existence of both natural and spiritual bodies in a human being.

2 Corinthians 7:1 - "Since we have these promises, dear friends, let us purify ourselves from everything that contaminates body and spirit, perfecting holiness out of reverence for God."

Jeremiah 9:25 - "The days are coming, declares the Lord, when I will punish all who are circumcised only in the flesh."

That is, circumcision of the heart, by the Spirit, is what we need.

James 2:26 reads:

"As the body without the spirit is dead, so faith without deeds is dead."

TONING THE SPIRIT USING THE BODY.

Take a look at Romans 12:1-2:

> *"Therefore, I urge you, brothers, in view of God's mercy, to offer your bodies as living sacrifices, holy and pleasing to God - this is your spiritual act of worship.*
> *² Do not conform any longer to the pattern of this world, but be transformed by the renewing of your mind. Then you will be able to test and approve what God's will is - his good, pleasing and perfect will."*

If double or even the same effort we put into keeping fit and staying healthy is exerted into presenting our bodies as a living sacrifice, then the result will be invaluable. Remember that good looks cannot take you to the Kingdom of God and you cannot muscle your way in. *'Therefore honour God with your body.'* (1 Corinthians 6:20).

TRAIN FOR THE IMPERISHABLE

Let us run with endurance the race that is set before us. Let us throw off everything that hinders and the sin that so easily entangles. Run the race with perseverance (Hebrews 12:1). Just like the apostle Paul, discipline the body, for:

> "²⁵ *Everyone who competes in the games goes into strict training. They do it to get a crown that will not last; but we do it to get a crown that will last for ever.*
> ²⁶ *Therefore I do not run like a man running aimlessly; I do not fight like a man beating the air.*
> ²⁷ *No, I beat my body and make it my slave so that after I have preached to others, I myself will not be disqualified for the prize."*
> — 1 Corinthians 9:25-27

I have discovered a better way to get a healthy body. Listen to this:

> *"Do not be wise in your own eyes; fear the Lord and shun evil. This will bring health to your body and nourishment to your bones."*
> — Proverbs 3:7-8

Train yourself to be godly. Get a six pack (rock-hard abs) as well as a nine pack (fruit of the Holy Spirit). Both can co-exist in you.

Change of Nationality

When one is faced with a life-threatening situation, in some cases, it takes God a long time to act when beseeched for help. And when he does answer, the outcome may be breathtaking. Ordinarily, you would change your nationality when you live in a foreign land and have satisfied certain requirements, but that was not the case with some people in all the provinces of King Xerxes.

The worst thing to do when faced with a life-threatening situation is to do nothing. Listen to this,

> "...call on me in the day of trouble; I will deliver you, and you will honour me." - Psalm 50:15.

Imagine that a group of people live in a foreign country, and a highly placed indigene of that country hated them. Because of the hatred, this indigenous person sought the king's order to destroy all of them. A decree to kill the foreigners was signed by the king. The situation just described was what Mordecai and the Jews faced in the hands of Haman under King Xerxes. When Mordecai saw a copy of the decree signed to kill all the Jews in the provinces of King Xerxes, Mordecai sent a message to Esther, his cousin, who was the queen, to beg the king to have pity on her people, the Jews. Esther was shown the decree and her reply to Mordecai meant she would do nothing concerning Mordecai's request. She said, "Anyone who goes in to see the king without being invited by him will be put to death." Esther's reply did not please Mordecai so he sent back this answer:

> *"Do not think that because you are in the king's house you alone of all the Jews will escape.* ¹⁴ *For if you remain silent at this time, relief and deliverance for the Jews will arise from another place, but you and your father's family will perish. And who knows but that you have come to your royal position for such a time as this?"*
>
> - Esther 4:13-14

Would you fast for three days, without eating and drinking, for an audience with a very important personality? That was what Esther, Mordecai, and the Jews in Susa did so that Esther could approach the king. The Lord answered their prayer and surprisingly, on the third day when Esther approached the king, the king asked, "What is it, Queen Esther? What is your request? Even up to half the kingdom, it will be given you." That was favour, and subsequently, the order to kill the Jews was overturned at Esther's request. Sometimes, to change a situation, all you need is an opportunity to speak to someone who is highly placed. The king issued an edict on behalf of the Jews giving them the right "to assemble and protect themselves; to destroy, kill and annihilate the armed men of any nationality or province who might attack them and their women and children, and to plunder the property of their enemies." For this reason:

> "In every province and in every city to which the edict of the king came, there was joy and gladness among the Jews, with feasting and celebrating. And **many people of other nationalities became Jews** because fear of the Jews had seized them." - Esther 8:17

Another death order similar to the aforementioned was overturned through Daniel's intervention. When King Nebuchadnezzar's counsellors, advisors, magicians, and wise men were unable to interpret his dream, he was so angry that he gave orders for every wise man in Babylonia to be put to death, including Daniel and his three friends. Daniel wisely sought an opportunity to speak to King Nebuchadnezzar so as to stop the death order.

Why I Don't Like God...

Take a look at the world around you. Today, a level of attainment or a degree of moral conduct is required to get to certain heights. It is a world where only the best will do. In the labour market, employers seek the best candidates to fill top positions in their establishments. Regarding matrimony, bachelors look for the most beautiful women to marry and damsels have well-to-do men on their list of eligible mates. To compete, racehorse owners want thoroughbreds in their stables and when choosing a place to live, people desire to have properties in the affluent areas of the city. But God uses a different selection method when choosing because his thoughts are nothing like our thoughts.

Imagine this! In 2007, the Information Commissioner's Office (ICO) in the United Kingdom uncovered that the Humberside Police Authority still had a record of the theft of 99 pence worth of meat by a youth in 1984. The record was kept for twenty-three years. Regardless of when committed, infidelity also has no place in politics today. The tabloid presses continue to dig for dirt so as to render a prospective candidate ineligible. Only people with a squeaky-clean image will do, but are all effective in the control and administration of public affairs?

When appointing leaders, God may not consider criminal

records nor would he take into account immigration status or one's status in the community.

Is God unjust? He chose a murderer (Moses), one not eloquent in speech, to lead Israel; the son of a harlot (Jephthah) captained Israel; an adulterer (David) fathered the richest and wisest man (Solomon) who ever lived and the former was the forefather of our Lord Jesus Christ. A shepherd boy (David) became a king, a foreigner (Esther) became a queen, and another foreigner (Joseph) became King Pharaoh's deputy. He hardened the heart of another Pharaoh, who did not know about Joseph, so he (God) could display his power and spread his fame throughout the whole world. A prostitute (Rahab) and her entire family were spared whilst others in the city (Jericho) they lived in perished. God authorised the evil adversary of humanity (Satan) who mercilessly afflicted a blameless man (Job) but with compassion restored twice the value of all that Job lost. Saul, who persecuted the Christians, became an apostle of Christ; a servant (Elisha) got double portion of his master's anointing; a ruler over Israel (Jesus) came from Bethlehem, a small clan of Judah; a man (Jesus) whose dad (God) owns all the properties on earth was born in a manger, an open box where feed for livestock is placed, and the same man rode on an ass, an inferior means of transportation when compared to the limousine equivalent of his time. Also, God empowered a man (Gideon) whose clan was the weakest in Manasseh to save Israel. His Son (Christ) kept 'bad company'; he ate with sinners.

God did not fire the errant prophet (Jonah) for refusing to go on an errand to Nineveh; instead, he gave Jonah a second chance. He also showed compassion to the idol worshippers travelling with the errant prophet because they prayed to him for mercy. One of the two robbers crucified with his Son (Jesus) was assured of paradise and a deposed king (Nebuchadnezzar) was reinstated with even greater honour than before after seven years of living in the fields with wild animals and eating grass like cows. What's more, no one was allowed to take his throne. Also, Onesimus, a runaway slave, through Apostle Paul's plea, returned to his master as a fellow worker in Christ.

Without filling any adoption forms, God gave us his only Son. He instructed the Israelites leaving Egypt to borrow articles of silver and gold and fine clothing from the Egyptians but there is no record showing that the items borrowed were returned. Does it sound like I am aggrieved? Far from it. For the way God does his things, I do not like him; **I actually have a deep rapturous love for him** because it is impossible for anyone to understand his decisions and his ways. Did he not say,

> "Come now, let us reason together ... Though your sins are like scarlet, they shall be as white as snow; though they are red as crimson, they shall be like wool." - Isaiah 1:18

Hallelujah!!!

PRODUCTS BY THE SAME AUTHOR

Bible Quiz for Princes and Princesses by Segun Ibitoye
Copyright © 2013 by Olusegun Victor Ibitoye
ISBN 978-0-9568142-3-4 (Paperback)

Also available in
Chinese,
French,
German,
Portuguese,
Spanish,
and Russian

MOBILE APPS FOR SMARTPHONES AND TABLETS FLUENT IN 9 LANGUAGES; Arabic, Chinese, English, French, German, Italian, Portuguese, Spanish, and Russian.

3R Bible Quiz
Deluxe

3R Bible Quiz
Intermediate

3R Bible Quiz
Easy

DIGGING DEEP - BIBLE STUDY MADE EASY

MY NOTES

DIGGING DEEP - BIBLE STUDY MADE EASY

MY NOTES

DIGGING DEEP - BIBLE STUDY MADE EASY